The Future-Proof CIO: Navigating ITSM in the Age of AI, Automation, and Beyond

Saboor Mubarak

Foreward

For IT there is one thing you can always depend on – technologies will always advance and change. Emerging technologies such as Blockchain, IoT, AI, robotics, and others usher in welcome improvements, but also pose new management and operating risks. IT Service Management (ITSM) is about reducing risk, increasing productivity, lowering costs, and improving end-user satisfaction. Yet, how will ITSM work to support these technologies? Can ITSM keep up with them? What needs to change? What stays the same?

Effective management of IT services is critical for business success. Technology is playing an ever-increasing role in nearly all facets of the business. Unless these technologies can be effectively managed and operated, the benefits of these technologies will not be realized. While much has been written about emerging technologies, little of it addresses how these technologies can be operated and managed to ensure those benefits can be obtained.

Until now.

Saboor's book takes you on a journey from the evolution of ITSM into today's world of leading technologies from a management perspective. It covers all the bases from Governance to DevOps and management of leading technologies. It ends with strategies for future-proofing the IT organization and providing a CIO roadmap for the future.

Readers will find this especially helpful as a reliable guide as they navigate through their own challenges as their organization technology footprint modernizes and expands.

About the Author

Saboor Mubarak is a seasoned professional with over 14 years of experience in IT transformation governance, IT service management, business resiliency, risk management, and IT audit. His career spans prestigious roles in large-scale management consulting firms worldwide, demonstrating a profound expertise in leveraging technology for business excellence. Saboor holds an MBA from Amity University, a B.S. in Computer Systems Engineering from Central Pacific University UAE, and an Artificial Intelligence in Business certification from The Wharton School USA.

His technical proficiency is underpinned by a wide array of certifications, including ITIL V3 Expert, COBIT 2019, ISO 20000 LA, ISO 27001 LI, and many others. At KPMG Saudi Arabia, as an Associate Director of IT Advisory, he has been instrumental in driving revenue growth, managing multimillion-dollar engagements, and leading significant IT transformations. Saboor's dedication to advancing IT governance, strategy, and enterprise architecture has significantly contributed to the digital transformation journeys of numerous organizations in the Middle East. His leadership in implementing IT service management processes, achieving ISO standards certifications, and spearheading IT audits underscores his commitment to excellence and his ability to navigate the complex landscape of technology consulting.

A visionary in technology consulting, Saboor's vast expertise encompasses enterprise architecture, IT governance, cyber security, data governance, and regulatory compliance, among others. He has a proven track record of developing and implementing strategic IT solutions that align with business objectives, ensuring seamless operational efficiency and bolstering organizational resilience. His innovative approach to

IT strategy and governance has been pivotal in fostering business growth and operational excellence for his clients.

Table of Contents

For **"The Future-Proof CIO: Navigating ITSM in the Age of AI, Automation, and Beyond"**, a table of contents that outlines a comprehensive journey through ITSM adaptation, emerging technologies, leadership strategies, and practical applications would serve the book's purpose well. Here's a detailed table of contents:

Contents

- Integrating AI with existing IT infrastructure

Chapter 5: The Impact of Automation and RPA

- Streamlining operations
- Enhancing efficiency and accuracy

Chapter 6: Embracing General AI and Advanced Analytics

- Predictive analytics in ITSM
- Future potentials of General AI

Part III: Strategic Management and Governance

Chapter 7: Governance Strategies for a Digital World

- Aligning IT governance with corporate strategy
- Cybersecurity and risk management

Chapter 8: Enterprise Architecture in the Age of Digital Transformation

- Designing flexible IT architectures
- Case studies of successful transformations

Chapter 9: ITSM and Project Management

- Agile, Scrum, and Kanban in ITSM
- Balancing traditional and agile methodologies

Part IV: Operational Excellence through ITSM

Chapter 10: DevOps: A Synergistic Approach

- Principles of DevOps in ITSM

Glossary

1. **Artificial Intelligence (AI)**: The simulation of human intelligence in machines that are programmed to think and learn like humans. In ITSM, AI is used to automate decision-making processes, enhance customer service, and improve predictive analytics.

2. **Machine Learning (ML)**: A subset of AI focusing on the development of algorithms that enable computers to learn from and make decisions based on data, without being explicitly programmed for each task.

3. **Robotic Process Automation (RPA)**: The use of software bots to automate highly repetitive and routine tasks previously carried out by human workers. In ITSM, RPA streamlines operations, enhancing efficiency and accuracy.

4. **Blockchain**: A decentralized ledger technology that records transactions across a network of computers. Blockchain enhances transparency and security in digital transactions, including those within ITSM frameworks.

5. **Internet of Things (IoT)**: The interconnection via the Internet of computing devices embedded in everyday objects, enabling them to send and receive data. IoT technology in ITSM can improve service delivery and operational efficiency.

6. **Predictive Analytics**: The use of data, statistical algorithms, and machine learning techniques to identify the likelihood of future outcomes based on historical data. In ITSM, predictive analytics is used for incident prediction, capacity planning, and continuous service improvement.

7. **Cybersecurity**: The practice of protecting systems, networks, and programs from digital attacks. Cybersecurity strategies are integral to ITSM to ensure the protection of data and IT services.

8. **Governance**: The framework of policies, processes, and rules that ensures IT strategies align with business goals and that IT operations are conducted securely, efficiently, and in compliance with regulations.

9. **DevOps**: A set of practices that combines software development (Dev) and IT operations (Ops), aiming to shorten the system development life cycle and provide continuous delivery with high software quality. DevOps in ITSM promotes a collaborative and agile working environment.

10. **Service Integration and Management (SIAM)**: An approach to managing multiple service providers by integrating them to provide a single business-facing IT organization. SIAM enhances the efficiency and quality of IT service delivery in complex environments.

11. **Change Management**: The process of managing changes to IT services or systems, ensuring that methods and procedures are used efficiently to handle changes and minimize the impact on service quality.

12. **Artificial General Intelligence (AGI)**: The hypothetical ability of an AI system to understand, learn, and apply intelligence to solve any problem, much like a human being. AGI represents the future potential of AI to perform any intellectual task that a human can do, potentially transforming ITSM through autonomous operations and decision-making.

13. **Quantum Computing**: A type of computing that takes advantage of quantum phenomena like superposition and entanglement to perform operations on data. The future integration of quantum computing in ITSM could revolutionize data processing and analysis.

Foreword

For IT there is one thing you can always depend on – technologies will always advance and change. Emerging technologies such as Blockchain, IoT, AI, robotics, and others usher in welcome improvements, but also pose new management and operating risks. IT Service Management (ITSM) is about reducing risk, increasing productivity, lowering costs, and improving end-user satisfaction. Yet, how will ITSM work to support these technologies? Can ITSM keep up with them? What needs to change? What stays the same?

Effective management of IT services is critical for business success. Technology is playing an ever-increasing role in nearly all facets of the business. Unless these technologies can be effectively managed and operated, the benefits of these technologies will not be realized. While much has been written about emerging technologies, little of it addresses how these technologies can be operated and managed to ensure those benefits can be obtained.

Until now.

Saboor's book takes you on a journey from the evolution of ITSM into today's world of leading technologies from a management perspective. It covers all the bases from Governance to DevOps and management of leading technologies. It ends with strategies for future-proofing the IT organization and providing a CIO roadmap for the future.

Readers will find this especially helpful as a reliable guide as they navigate through their own challenges as their organization technology footprint modernizes and expands.

Welcome to the journey of becoming a Future-Proof CIO.

Randy Steinberg

19th March 2024

Preface

As the author of "The Future-Proof CIO: Navigating ITSM in the Age of AI, Automation, and Beyond," I embark on a journey to bridge the gap between the present challenges and future opportunities faced by Chief Information Officers (CIOs) and IT leaders in an era dominated by rapid technological advancements. This book is born out of a deep-seated belief that the future of IT service management (ITSM) lies in our ability to adapt, innovate, and embrace the transformative power of artificial intelligence (AI), automation, and other emerging technologies.

The role of the CIO has never been more critical or more challenging. In a landscape where digital transformation dictates the pace of business, IT leaders are tasked with steering their organizations through uncharted waters, balancing the need for innovation with the imperative of maintaining stability and security. This book is a response to those challenges, offering insights, strategies, and practical advice for navigating the complexities of ITSM in the digital age.

Drawing from my experiences, conversations with industry leaders, and extensive research, "The Future-Proof CIO" aims to provide a comprehensive overview of the current state of ITSM, the impact of AI and automation on the field, and the skills and strategies necessary for future-proofing one's career and organization. Each chapter is designed to offer valuable perspectives on how to leverage technology to drive business value, enhance operational efficiency, and foster a culture of innovation and agility.

This book also addresses the often overlooked aspect of leadership in the context of technological transformation. It emphasizes the importance of developing a visionary mindset, the capacity for strategic thinking, and the soft skills necessary to lead diverse and dynamic teams through periods of change.

The journey to becoming a future-proof CIO is fraught with challenges and uncertainties, but it is also filled with immense opportunities for growth, innovation, and leadership. It is my hope that this book serves as a guide for IT leaders at all levels, providing the knowledge, inspiration, and tools needed to navigate the future of ITSM with confidence and foresight.

As you turn these pages, I invite you to reflect on your own experiences, challenges, and aspirations. May you find within this book the insights and inspiration to lead with courage, innovate with purpose, and shape the future of your organization in the age of AI, automation, and beyond.

Welcome to the journey.

Saboor   Mubarak

Description

The Future-Proof CIO: Navigating ITSM in the Age of AI, Automation, and Beyond is a definitive guide for Chief Information Officers (CIOs), Chief Technology Officers (CTOs), and senior IT leaders poised to steer their organizations through the tumultuous waters of digital transformation. With a keen focus on the integration of emerging technologies within IT Service Management (ITSM), this book offers a strategic blueprint for creating resilient, agile, and future-ready IT infrastructures.

Spanning over eighteen meticulously crafted chapters, divided into six parts, the book embarks on a journey from the foundational aspects of ITSM in the digital era to the strategic management and governance needed to navigate future technological landscapes. It begins with an exploration of the evolving role of ITSM, offering historical context and a vision for its future, emphasizing the expanded responsibilities and strategic leadership roles of CIOs and CTOs in today's technology-driven enterprises.

The Future-Proof CIO delves deep into the core technologies that are reshaping ITSM, such as Artificial Intelligence (AI), Robotic Process Automation (RPA), and advanced analytics. Through practical applications and case studies, it illustrates how these technologies can streamline operations, enhance efficiency, and drive innovation. The book also addresses the integration challenges and opportunities presented by these technologies, providing actionable insights for leveraging them within existing IT infrastructures.

Strategic management and governance form the backbone of effective ITSM in the age of digital transformation. The book offers comprehensive strategies for aligning IT governance with corporate strategy, designing flexible enterprise architectures, and managing risk in a digitally transformed world. It also explores the synergies between ITSM and project management methodologies like Agile and DevOps, highlighting best practices for service integration and change management.

Leadership is at the heart of successful ITSM transformation. **The Future-Proof CIO** emphasizes visionary leadership, the cultivation of high-performance teams, and the fostering of innovation and creativity within IT organizations. It provides a roadmap for CIOs and IT leaders to guide their teams through digital transformation, overcome common pitfalls, and build a culture of continuous improvement and learning.

As it navigates towards the future landscape of ITSM, the book explores emerging trends and technologies, from quantum computing to edge computing, offering strategies for future-proofing IT organizations. It concludes with a forward-looking roadmap, equipping IT leaders with the knowledge, strategies, and confidence to lead their organizations into the future.

The Future-Proof CIO is not just a book; it's a companion for IT leaders who aspire to leverage emerging technologies to create innovative, resilient, and agile IT services. It combines theoretical insights with practical guidance, making it an indispensable resource for navigating the complexities of ITSM in the digital age.

Part I: Foundations of Future-Proof ITSM

Chapter 1: The Evolution of IT Service Management

Historical Context

The evolution of IT Service Management (ITSM) is a narrative of adaptation and advancement, mirroring the rapid development and integration of information technology in business operations. Initially, IT functions were relegated to the back-office, focusing predominantly on hardware and software maintenance without a cohesive approach to service management. This disjointed method often resulted in inefficiencies and a reactive stance toward IT issues.

The Genesis of ITIL and Standardization

The landscape of ITSM began to transform with the introduction of the Information Technology Infrastructure Library (ITIL) in the 1980s by the UK's Central Computer and Telecommunications Agency (CCTA). ITIL was groundbreaking in that it offered a set of standardized best practices for IT service management, emphasizing efficiency, consistency, and alignment with business goals. This marked the beginning of ITSM's journey from a fragmented IT approach to a structured and strategic endeavor.

ITIL's methodologies revolved around the lifecycle of IT services, encompassing service strategy, design, transition, operation, and continual improvement. This lifecycle approach not only streamlined IT operations but also ensured that IT services evolved in tandem with changing business requirements.

Broadening the ITSM Framework

Following the success of ITIL, other frameworks and standards emerged to augment ITSM practices. ISO/IEC 20000 set international standards for IT service management, while COBIT provided a comprehensive framework for IT governance, focusing on regulatory compliance, risk management, and strategic alignment. These frameworks, alongside ITIL, equipped organizations with robust methodologies for effective IT service management.

ITSM in the Digital Age

The onset of the digital age heralded significant changes for ITSM, driven by digital transformation and the proliferation of emerging technologies. This era demanded a reevaluation of traditional ITSM practices to accommodate the dynamic nature of digital business models.

Embracing Emerging Technologies

Technological advancements such as cloud computing, artificial intelligence (AI), machine learning (ML), and the Internet of Things (IoT) have fundamentally altered the ITSM landscape. These technologies introduced new capabilities for automating processes, enhancing decision-making with predictive analytics, and offering scalable and flexible IT services. Modern ITSM strategies incorporate these technologies to improve service efficiency, responsiveness, and innovation.

Agile and DevOps Integration

The digital age also emphasized the importance of agility and collaboration in IT service management. Agile methodologies, with their focus on flexibility and customer feedback, and DevOps practices, which bridge the gap between software development and IT operations, have significantly influenced ITSM. By integrating Agile and DevOps, ITSM has become more adaptive, enabling faster and more efficient delivery of IT services that better meet the needs of the business and its customers. The Agile and DevOps integration is explained with the help of the diagram below:

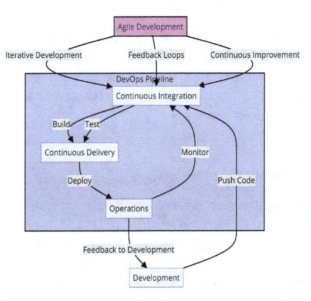

The diagram showcases how Agile development methodologies seamlessly integrate with the DevOps pipeline, emphasizing continuous improvement, feedback, and delivery.

1. **Agile Development**: This is the starting point, where Agile methodologies prioritize iterative development, feedback loops, and continuous improvement. These practices ensure that development is aligned with customer needs and can adapt to changes rapidly.

2. **Continuous Integration (CI)**: Agile development feeds into Continuous Integration, where the code produced during Agile sprints is frequently integrated into a shared repository. This stage includes building the code and running tests to ensure that new changes integrate well with the existing codebase.

3. **Continuous Delivery (CD)**: After CI, the code moves to Continuous Delivery, where it is automatically deployed to a testing or staging environment. This ensures that the code is always in a deployable state, facilitating quick releases.

4. **Operations (Ops)**: The Operations stage involves deploying the code to production, monitoring its performance, and gathering feedback from users.

5. **Feedback to Development**: Feedback from operations and users is crucial for Agile development. This loop ensures that the development process continually improves and adapts based on real-world use.

6. **DevOps Pipeline**: The entire flow from Agile development through CI, CD, and Operations, with feedback loops back to development, forms the integrated Agile-DevOps pipeline. This illustrates how development and operations are no longer siloed but work together to improve speed, efficiency, and quality in software development and deployment.

The highlighted integration points between Agile and DevOps underline the synergy between these methodologies, emphasizing continuous improvement and responsiveness to change.

A Customer-Centric Focus

Today, ITSM is increasingly oriented toward delivering value and enhancing the customer experience. In the digital age, IT services are not just support mechanisms but vital components of the customer value proposition. This shift has led to a more customer centric ITSM approach, where services are designed and managed with the end-user experience in mind. Feedback mechanisms and continuous improvement processes ensure that IT services remain aligned with customer needs and expectations.

Future Directions

As ITSM continues to evolve, it will face new challenges and opportunities presented by advancing technology and changing business landscapes. The integration of artificial intelligence and automation will further transform IT service delivery, making services more proactive and personalized. Meanwhile, the ongoing shift towards cloud and as-a-service models will require ITSM to manage and govern a more complex and distributed IT ecosystem.

Furthermore, the importance of cybersecurity and data protection within ITSM will increase, necessitating integrated risk management and governance practices. The future of ITSM lies in its ability to adapt to these changes, leveraging technology not only to improve service delivery but also to drive business innovation and growth.

Conclusion

The journey of IT Service Management from its foundational years to the present digital era is a testament to the evolving role of IT in business. From operational support to strategic partnership, ITSM has adapted to meet the needs of a rapidly changing technological and business environment. As organizations continue to navigate the complexities of digital transformation, the principles and practices of ITSM will remain crucial in aligning IT capabilities with business objectives and delivering value in an increasingly digital world.

Questions and Answers

Q1. What initiated the evolution of IT Service Management (ITSM)?

Answer: The evolution of ITSM was initiated by the rapid development and integration of information technology in business operations. Initially, IT functions focused mainly on hardware and software maintenance without a cohesive service management approach, leading to inefficiencies and a reactive stance toward IT issues.

Q2. How did the introduction of ITIL transform ITSM?

Answer: ITIL, introduced in the 1980s by the UK's Central Computer and Telecommunications Agency (CCTA), was groundbreaking for ITSM. It provided a set of standardized best practices that emphasized efficiency, consistency, and business goal alignment. ITIL marked the transition from fragmented IT approaches to a structured, strategic endeavor, revolving around the lifecycle of IT services and ensuring their evolution in tandem with changing business requirements.

Q3. What role did frameworks like ISO/IEC 20000 and COBIT play in ITSM?

Answer: Following ITIL's success, frameworks like ISO/IEC 20000 and COBIT emerged to augment ITSM practices. ISO/IEC 20000 set international standards for IT service management, while COBIT offered a comprehensive framework for IT governance, focusing on regulatory compliance, risk management, and strategic alignment. These frameworks provided organizations with robust methodologies for effective IT service management.

Q4. How have emerging technologies influenced ITSM in the digital age?

Answer: The advent of cloud computing, AI, machine learning, and IoT has fundamentally changed the ITSM landscape by introducing capabilities for process automation, enhanced decision-making through predictive analytics, and scalable, flexible IT services. Modern ITSM strategies now incorporate these technologies to improve service efficiency, responsiveness, and innovation.

Q5. In what ways has ITSM become more customer-centric in the digital age?

Answer: In the digital age, ITSM has shifted towards delivering value and enhancing the customer experience, recognizing IT services as vital components of the customer value proposition. This customer-centric approach involves designing and managing services with the end-user experience in mind, using feedback mechanisms and continuous improvement processes to ensure alignment with customer needs and expectations.

Q6. What future challenges and opportunities does ITSM face?

Answer: ITSM faces challenges and opportunities from advancing technology and changing business landscapes, including the need to adapt to artificial intelligence, automation, cloud, and as-a-service models. The importance of cybersecurity and data protection is also increasing, necessitating integrated risk management and governance practices. The future of ITSM lies in its ability to leverage technology to improve service delivery and drive business innovation and growth.

Q7. How has the role of ITSM changed from its early years to the present?

Answer: ITSM has evolved from a role of operational support to a strategic partnership within businesses. This evolution reflects the changing technological and business environment, with ITSM adapting to meet the needs of rapid digital transformation. The principles and practices of ITSM remain crucial for aligning IT capabilities with business objectives and delivering value in an increasingly digital world.

These Q&As offer a comprehensive view of ITSM's evolution, its current state, and future directions, highlighting the critical role of technology and strategic management in delivering efficient and aligned IT services.

Case Study

The Evolution of IT Service Management

Introduction:

This case study explores the evolution of IT Service Management (ITSM) through its historical context, the genesis of ITIL and standardization, the broadening of the ITSM framework, and its transformation in the digital age. It also discusses the current customer-centric focus of ITSM and anticipates future directions for this critical field.

Historical Context:

In the early days of IT, organizations primarily viewed IT functions as back-office support, with a focus on hardware and software maintenance. The lack of a cohesive approach often resulted in a reactive stance toward IT issues, leading to inefficiencies and operational challenges.

Genesis of ITIL and Standardization:

The transformation of ITSM began with the introduction of ITIL in the 1980s. Developed by the UK's Central Computer and Telecommunications Agency (CCTA), ITIL provided a standardized set of best practices for IT service management. This marked the shift from a fragmented IT approach to a structured and strategic endeavor. ITIL's emphasis on efficiency, consistency, and alignment with business goals laid the foundation for modern ITSM practices. It introduced the concept of the IT service lifecycle, including service strategy, design, transition, operation, and continual improvement.

Broadening the ITSM Framework:

Following the success of ITIL, other frameworks and standards such as ISO/IEC 20000 and COBIT emerged. These frameworks supplemented ITSM practices, setting international standards for IT service management and offering comprehensive governance and compliance guidelines. Organizations now had access to robust methodologies to enhance their IT service management capabilities.

ITSM in the Digital Age:

The advent of the digital age brought about significant changes in ITSM. Digital transformation and emerging technologies necessitated a reevaluation of traditional ITSM practices to accommodate the dynamic nature of digital business models.

Embracing Emerging Technologies:

Technological advancements like cloud computing, artificial intelligence (AI), machine learning (ML), and the Internet of Things (IoT) introduced new capabilities to ITSM. These technologies enabled automation, predictive analytics, scalability, and flexibility, enhancing service efficiency, responsiveness, and innovation.

Agile and DevOps Integration:

Agile methodologies and DevOps practices influenced ITSM by emphasizing flexibility, collaboration, and customer feedback. Integration of these approaches led to an adaptive ITSM environment, facilitating faster and more efficient delivery of IT services aligned with business and customer needs.

A Customer-Centric Focus:

In the digital age, ITSM has shifted its focus towards delivering value and enhancing the customer experience. II services are no longer mere support mechanisms but essential components of the customer value proposition. A customer centric ITSM approach ensures that services are designed and managed with the end-user experience in mind, with continuous improvement processes and feedback mechanisms in place to meet customer expectations.

Future Directions:

As ITSM continues to evolve, it faces new challenges and opportunities. Integration of AI and automation will further transform service delivery, making it proactive and personalized. The shift toward cloud and as-a-service models will require ITSM to manage a more complex and distributed IT ecosystem. Cybersecurity and data protection will become increasingly crucial, necessitating integrated risk management and governance practices.

Conclusion:

The journey of IT Service Management from its early days to the present digital era showcases the evolving role of IT in business. From operational support to strategic partnership, ITSM has adapted to meet the needs of a rapidly changing technological and business environment. As organizations navigate digital transformation, the principles, and practices of ITSM will remain crucial in aligning IT capabilities with business objectives and delivering value in an increasingly digital world. ITSM's continued evolution will enable organizations to embrace technological advancements and drive business innovation and growth.

Exercise:

Try answering the following questions based on your reading of the above case study.

1. What were the primary challenges faced by IT professionals during the early days of ITSM, and how did these challenges impact IT operations?

2. How did the introduction of ITIL in the 1980s mark a significant turning point in the history of ITSM, and what were the key principles it introduced?

3. Describe the components of the IT service lifecycle as outlined by ITIL. How did this lifecycle approach transform ITSM practices?

4. What role did standardization play in the evolution of ITSM, and how did frameworks like ISO/IEC 20000 and COBIT contribute to the industry?

5. In the digital age, what are the main technological advancements that have reshaped ITSM practices, and how have they improved service efficiency and innovation?

6. How has the integration of Agile methodologies and DevOps practices influenced ITSM, and why is this integration important for modern IT service delivery?

7. Explain the shift towards a customer-centric focus in ITSM during the digital age. How has this shift impacted the way IT services are designed and managed?

8. What are the anticipated future directions for ITSM, and how will emerging technologies like AI, automation, and cloud computing shape its evolution?

9. What challenges and opportunities do you foresee for IT professionals as ITSM continues to adapt and evolve in the digital era?

10. How can IT professionals ensure that ITSM remains aligned with business objectives and continues to deliver value in an increasingly digital world?

Chapter 2: The Role of CIOs and CTOs Today

In the rapidly evolving landscape of technology and business, the roles of Chief Information Officers (CIOs) and Chief Technology Officers (CTOs) have become increasingly pivotal. As organizations navigate through digital transformation, cybersecurity threats, and the integration of emerging technologies, the responsibilities of CIOs and CTOs have expanded and evolved. This chapter delves into the contemporary roles of these executives, shedding light on their strategic importance in driving business growth, fostering innovation, and ensuring operational excellence.

Introduction to the Roles

The CIO's role traditionally focuses on the management, implementation, and usability of information and computer technologies. Their main objective is to leverage technology to fulfill the organization's strategic goals, streamline operations, and improve the overall efficiency of business processes. On the other hand, the CTO primarily focuses on external technology trends, aligning the company's product and technology strategy with its business goals. They play a critical role in product development, technology vision setting, and innovation management.

1. **Driving Digital Transformation**: A notable example of a CIO leading digital transformation is at a global retail giant. The CIO spearheaded the adoption of cloud computing, artificial intelligence (AI), and machine learning (ML) to enhance customer experience, improve supply chain efficiency, and increase sales. This initiative not only streamlined operations but also significantly boosted the company's market competitiveness.

2. **Fostering Innovation and Product Development**: A leading technology firm's CTO was instrumental in developing a groundbreaking AI-driven product that revolutionized the market. By closely monitoring emerging technologies and fostering a culture of innovation within the team, the CTO led the development of a product that not only met the current market demand but also set new industry standards.

3. **Enhancing Cybersecurity Measures**: In the financial sector, a CIO's strategic approach to cybersecurity has been pivotal in safeguarding sensitive customer information and maintaining trust. By implementing advanced security protocols, conducting regular audits, and fostering a culture of security awareness, the CIO ensured that the organization remained resilient against increasing cybersecurity threats.

4. **Leading IT Infrastructure Overhaul**: A CTO at a manufacturing company led a complete overhaul of the IT infrastructure to support the adoption of the Internet of Things (IoT) and smart manufacturing processes. This strategic move not only improved operational efficiency but also significantly reduced downtime and maintenance costs, leading to higher productivity and profitability.

5. **Cultivating Partnerships and Ecosystems**: A CIO in the healthcare industry successfully cultivated partnerships with technology providers and other healthcare institutions to develop a shared digital health platform. This platform facilitated the exchange of patient data in a secure manner, improving patient care quality and operational efficiency across the ecosystem.

Expanding Responsibilities

The digital age has ushered in a new era for CIOs and CTOs, expanding their responsibilities far beyond the traditional scope. Today, they are instrumental in driving digital transformation, enhancing cybersecurity, managing data governance, fostering innovation, and leading talent management initiatives.

Digital Transformation Leadership

CIOs and CTOs are the architects of digital transformation, guiding their organizations through the integration of digital technology into all areas of business. This transformation is not just about technology implementation but also about fundamentally changing how businesses operate and deliver value to customers. It involves a cultural change that requires these leaders to challenge the status quo, experiment, and get comfortable with failure.

Cybersecurity and Data Governance

As cyber threats become more sophisticated, the role of CIOs and CTOs in cybersecurity has become more critical. They are tasked with developing and implementing comprehensive cybersecurity strategies to protect organizational assets while ensuring compliance with evolving data protection regulations. This responsibility includes overseeing risk management practices, developing incident response plans, and ensuring the ethical use of data.

Innovation and Agility

Innovation is at the heart of the expanded role of CIOs and CTOs. They are expected to foster a culture of innovation within their organizations, encouraging experimentation and the adoption of agile methodologies. This not only speeds up the development process but also helps organizations remain flexible and responsive to market changes and customer needs.

Talent Management and Skills Development

The technology landscape is evolving rapidly, creating a pressing need for skilled IT professionals. CIOs and CTOs are deeply involved in talent management, focusing on recruiting, retaining, and developing the right talent to meet current and future technological challenges. This includes identifying skill gaps, advocating for continuous learning, and building teams that can innovate and adapt to new technologies.

Strategic Leadership in Technology

Strategic leadership in technology requires CIOs and CTOs to align IT strategies with business objectives, drive customer-centric innovation, and prepare the organization for future technological shifts.

Aligning IT and Business Strategies

Effective CIOs and CTOs ensure that IT strategies are not only aligned with but also actively support the organization's business goals. This involves working closely with other business leaders to understand their needs and how technology can solve existing problems or create new business opportunities. Strategic alignment helps in prioritizing IT projects, optimizing technology investments, and measuring the impact of IT on business outcomes.

Customer-Centric Innovation

CIOs and CTOs play a key role in leveraging technology to enhance the customer experience. This involves using data analytics to gain insights into customer behavior, preferences, and trends. By understanding the customer journey, IT leaders can implement technologies that personalize the customer experience, streamline interactions, and build stronger relationships with customers.

Preparing for Future Technological Shifts

With the rapid pace of technological innovation, CIOs and CTOs must keep an eye on the horizon, anticipating and preparing for future shifts. This includes exploring emerging technologies such as artificial intelligence, blockchain, and Internet of Things (IoT) for their potential to disrupt or transform the industry. Strategic leadership involves not only recognizing these opportunities but also evaluating their feasibility, potential ROI, and alignment with the organization's long-term goals.

Conclusion

The role of CIOs and CTOs has expanded significantly, placing them at the heart of business strategy and innovation. Their ability to navigate the complexities of the digital age, drive transformational change, and align technology with business goals is critical for organizational success. As strategic leaders, they must continue to evolve, adapt, and inspire their teams to harness the power of technology to create sustainable competitive advantages and drive future growth.

Questions and Answers

Q1: How have the roles of CIOs and CTOs evolved in the contemporary business landscape?

Answer: The roles of CIOs and CTOs have evolved dramatically from overseeing IT infrastructure and operations to becoming central figures in crafting and executing business strategies. They leverage technology for competitive advantage, driving digital transformation, enhancing cybersecurity, managing data governance, fostering innovation, and leading talent management initiatives.

Q2: What is meant by "digital transformation leadership" in the context of the roles of CIOs and CTOs?

Answer: Digital transformation leadership refers to the role of CIOs and CTOs as architects of digital transformation, guiding their organizations through the integration of digital technology into all business areas. This involves fundamentally changing how businesses operate and deliver value to customers, requiring a cultural shift towards challenging the status quo, experimentation, and comfort with failure.

Q3: Why has the role of CIOs and CTOs in cybersecurity become more critical?

Answer: With the increasing sophistication of cyber threats, CIOs and CTOs are tasked with developing comprehensive cybersecurity strategies to protect organizational assets and ensure compliance with evolving data protection regulations. Their role includes overseeing risk management practices, developing incident response plans, and ensuring the ethical use of data.

Q4: How do CIOs and CTOs foster a culture of innovation and agility within their organizations?

Answer: CIOs and CTOs foster a culture of innovation by encouraging experimentation and adopting agile methodologies. This approach speeds up the development process and helps organizations remain flexible and responsive to market changes and customer needs, ensuring continuous innovation and adaptability.

Q5: What role do CIOs and CTOs play in talent management and skills development?

Answer: CIOs and CTOs are deeply involved in talent management, focusing on recruiting, retaining, and developing the right talent to meet technological challenges. They identify skill gaps, advocate for continuous learning, and build teams capable of innovating and adapting to new technologies.

Q6: How do CIOs and CTOs align IT strategies with business objectives?

Answer: CIOs and CTOs ensure that IT strategies actively support the organization's business goals by working closely with other business leaders. This strategic alignment involves understanding business needs, solving problems with technology, prioritizing IT projects, optimizing technology investments, and measuring the impact of IT on business outcomes.

Q7: In what ways do CIOs and CTOs enhance the customer experience through technology?

Answer: CIOs and CTOs enhance the customer experience by using data analytics to gain insights into customer behavior and preferences. They implement technologies that personalize the customer experience, streamline interactions, and build stronger customer relationships, focusing on understanding and improving the customer journey.

Q8: How do CIOs and CTOs prepare their organizations for future technological shifts?

Answer: CIOs and CTOs keep an eye on emerging technologies such as AI, blockchain, and IoT, evaluating their potential to disrupt or transform the industry. They prepare for future shifts by recognizing opportunities, assessing feasibility and potential ROI, and ensuring alignment with the organization's long-term goals.

Q9: Why is the expanded role of CIOs and CTOs critical for organizational success?

Answer: The expanded role of CIOs and CTOs is critical for organizational success because they navigate the complexities of the digital age, drive transformational change, and align technology with business goals. Their strategic leadership is essential for creating sustainable competitive advantages and driving future growth.

Case Study - The Evolving Roles of CIOs and CTOs in Modern Business

Introduction:

Chapter 2 of this book explores how the roles of Chief Information Officers (CIOs) and Chief Technology Officers (CTOs) have evolved significantly in contemporary business landscapes. It highlights their expanding responsibilities and their pivotal roles in strategic leadership in technology.

Expanding Responsibilities:

Over the years, the responsibilities of CIOs and CTOs have extended far beyond their traditional roles in managing IT infrastructure and operations. They now play integral roles in shaping various aspects of an organization's strategic direction.

Digital Transformation Leadership:

CIOs and CTOs have emerged as leaders in spearheading digital transformation initiatives within their organizations. They are responsible for orchestrating efforts to integrate digital technology across all aspects of the business. This includes not only the implementation of technological solutions but also fostering a cultural shift that encourages innovation, experimentation, and adaptability.

Cybersecurity and Data Governance:

In an era of escalating cyber threats and evolving data protection regulations, CIOs and CTOs have taken on crucial responsibilities in ensuring the security and ethical handling of data within their organizations. They develop and implement comprehensive cybersecurity strategies, oversee risk management practices, and are vigilant in responding to incidents while upholding data governance standards.

Innovation and Agility:

A significant aspect of their evolving roles centers on cultivating a culture of innovation and agility within the organization. CIOs and CTOs encourage cross-functional teams to explore emerging technologies, experiment with new ideas, and adopt agile methodologies. This shift in mindset not only accelerates the development process but also enhances an organization's adaptability to changing market dynamics.

Talent Management and Skills Development:

Recognizing the dynamic nature of the technology landscape, CIOs and CTOs are deeply involved in talent management and skills development. They prioritize recruiting, retaining, and nurturing IT professionals who possess the necessary expertise to address current and future technological challenges. This entails identifying skill gaps, advocating for continuous learning, and cultivating teams capable of innovating and adapting to evolving technologies.

Strategic Leadership in Technology:

The strategic leadership role of CIOs and CTOs is central to their evolving responsibilities. They align IT strategies with overarching business objectives, forging a strong connection between technology and organizational success. This alignment involves collaborating closely with other business leaders, understanding their needs, and leveraging technology to solve problems, drive growth, and enhance the customer experience.

Conclusion:

In conclusion, the roles of CIOs and CTOs have undergone significant transformations in response to the rapidly changing technological landscape. Their expanding responsibilities encompass leadership in digital transformation, cybersecurity, data governance, innovation, talent management, and strategic alignment of technology with business goals. As strategic leaders in technology, CIOs and CTOs are instrumental in guiding organizations toward sustainable growth and success in the digital age.

Exercise:

Try answering the following questions based on your reading of the above case study.

1. How have the roles of CIOs and CTOs evolved beyond traditional IT management, as described in the case study?

2. Can you explain the concept of digital transformation leadership and how CIOs and CTOs are instrumental in driving this transformation within organizations?

3. What are the key responsibilities of CIOs and CTOs in the context of cybersecurity and data governance, as discussed in the case study?

4. How do CIOs and CTOs foster a culture of innovation and agility within their organizations, and why is this cultural shift important in the digital age?

5. What challenges do CIOs and CTOs face in talent management and skills development, and how do they address these challenges to ensure their teams remain competitive?

6. Describe the strategic leadership role of CIOs and CTOs in aligning IT strategies with business objectives. Why is this alignment crucial for organizational success?

7. In your opinion, which of the expanded responsibilities discussed in the case study is the most critical for CIOs and CTOs in the current business landscape, and why?

8. How can aspiring CIOs and CTOs prepare themselves to excel in their roles as strategic technology leaders, given the dynamic nature of technology and business, as portrayed in the case study?

9. Can you provide examples of organizations or industries where CIOs and CTOs have played a transformative role in their evolving responsibilities, resulting in significant positive outcomes?

10. What role do you believe CIOs and CTOs will continue to play in shaping the future of businesses as technology continues to advance?

Chapter 3: Overview of Emerging Technologies

In the ever-evolving tapestry of technological advancement, certain innovations stand out, heralding a new era of digital transformation. This chapter delves into the core of these emerging technologies—Artificial Intelligence (AI), Machine Learning (ML) and their subsets, Robotic Process Automation (RPA), Blockchain, and the Internet of Things (IoT)—each representing a cornerstone of modern digital strategies. As we explore these technologies, we uncover their principles, applications, and the transformative potential they hold for industries and society at large.

Artificial Intelligence (AI) and Machine Learning (ML)

At the heart of the new technological revolution lie AI and ML, two interwoven disciplines reshaping the fabric of how decisions are made and operations are conducted. AI, with its broad ambit, encompasses the development of computer systems capable of performing tasks that typically require human intelligence. These tasks include speech recognition, decision-making, visual perception, and language translation. Machine Learning, a crucial subset of AI, focuses on creating algorithms that enable computers to learn and make decisions from data without being explicitly programmed.

Subsets of Machine Learning:

- **Deep Learning:** A subset of ML, deep learning utilizes neural networks with multiple layers (hence the term "deep") to analyze vast amounts of data. These networks mimic the human brain's structure, making deep learning particularly adept at processing complex data sets for image and speech recognition, among other tasks.

- **Natural Language Processing (NLP):** NLP allows machines to understand and interpret human language, enabling applications such as chatbots, sentiment analysis, and automated translation services.

Robotic Process Automation (RPA)

RPA stands as a beacon of operational efficiency, automating repetitive and rule-based tasks that have traditionally consumed the valuable time of human employees. By mimicking human actions in interacting with digital systems and software, RPA bots can handle tasks ranging from data entry and processing to complex transaction handling. This automation not only boosts efficiency but also allows human workers to focus on more strategic and creative tasks, driving innovation and growth.

Blockchain

Blockchain technology, often associated with cryptocurrencies like Bitcoin, offers far more in terms of security, transparency, and efficiency in digital transactions. At its core, blockchain is a decentralized ledger that records all transactions across a network of computers. This decentralization ensures that no single entity can control or tamper with the data, making blockchain an ideal solution for applications requiring high levels of trust and security, such as financial transactions, supply chain management, and identity verification.

Internet of Things (IoT)

IoT represents a significant shift towards a more interconnected and intelligent world, where physical objects are embedded with sensors, software, and other technologies to connect and exchange data with other devices and systems over the Internet. This interconnectedness opens up new avenues for optimizing processes, enhancing customer experiences, and creating value in ways previously unimaginable. From smart homes and wearable devices to intelligent industrial equipment,

IoT is paving the way for a more efficient, responsive, and data-driven world.

Beyond: The Frontier of Innovation

As we look beyond the current technological landscape, emerging frontiers such as quantum computing, augmented reality (AR), virtual reality (VR), and edge computing promise to further expand the boundaries of what's possible. These technologies, while still in their nascent stages, hold the potential to revolutionize fields such as computing, entertainment, manufacturing, and healthcare, offering new dimensions of interaction, processing power, and operational efficiency.

In conclusion, the journey through the landscape of emerging technologies is one of continuous exploration and discovery. For businesses, governments, and individuals alike, understanding and embracing these technologies is crucial for navigating the challenges and opportunities of the digital age. As we forge ahead, the integration of AI, ML, RPA, blockchain, IoT, and beyond into our digital strategies will not only drive innovation and growth but also shape the future of our global society.

Questions and Answers

1. How can AI and ML be strategically integrated into our business operations to drive innovation and efficiency?

- **Answer:** AI and ML can be strategically integrated into business operations by automating decision-making processes, enhancing customer service through personalized experiences, and improving predictive analytics for better decision-making. Identifying areas where data-driven insights can optimize operations, such as supply chain management or customer relationship management, can significantly drive innovation and efficiency.

2. What considerations should be made when implementing Deep Learning within our organization's existing technology infrastructure?

- **Answer:** When implementing Deep Learning, consider the computational resources required for training complex models, the availability and quality of data, and the integration with existing systems. Evaluating whether your current infrastructure can support these needs or if additional investments are necessary is crucial. Additionally, consider the expertise required to develop and maintain deep learning models, ensuring your team has the skills or providing training as needed.

3. In what ways can RPA transform our organization's workflow and productivity, and what are the typical challenges in its implementation?

- **Answer:** RPA can transform organizational workflow and productivity by automating repetitive tasks, reducing errors, and freeing up employees to focus on higher-value work. Challenges in implementation include selecting the right processes for automation, managing changes in workflow, ensuring data security, and training employees to work alongside RPA technologies. A clear strategy and governance model can help address these challenges.

4. How does Blockchain technology offer solutions to data security and transparency challenges in our organization?

- **Answer:** Blockchain technology offers solutions to data security and transparency challenges by providing a decentralized and tamper-proof ledger for recording transactions. This ensures that data integrity is maintained, and all transactions are transparent and verifiable by all parties involved. Implementing blockchain can enhance trust in data management, especially in areas like supply chains, contracts, and secure transactions.

5. What are the strategic benefits of integrating IoT into our products and services, and what security concerns should we address?

- **Answer:** Integrating IoT into products and services can provide strategic benefits such as enhanced data collection, improved customer experiences, and the development of new business models based on real-time insights. However, it also raises security concerns, including the protection of IoT devices from unauthorized access and ensuring the privacy and security of the data they collect. Implementing robust security protocols and regular security assessments are critical to address these concerns.

6. As we look beyond current technologies, what emerging trends should our organization prepare for to stay competitive?

- **Answer:** Organizations should prepare for trends such as quantum computing, which will revolutionize data processing power; augmented reality (AR) and virtual reality (VR), which will create new customer interaction platforms; and edge computing, which will enhance data processing speeds by bringing computation closer to data sources. Staying informed about these trends and investing in research and development can help your organization stay competitive.

7. How can we ensure our technology strategy remains aligned with business objectives amidst the rapid evolution of these emerging technologies?

- **Answer:** Ensuring your technology strategy remains aligned with business objectives requires continuous monitoring of technology trends, regular reviews of the technology strategy, and flexible planning that allows for quick adaptation to new innovations. Involving business leaders in technology decision-making processes and establishing cross-functional teams can also ensure that technology investments directly support business goals.

Case Study: Transforming Financial Services through Emerging Technologies

Background

In the rapidly evolving financial services sector, a leading institution sought to harness emerging technologies to stay ahead of the competition, enhance customer experience, and streamline operations. Recognizing the transformative potential of Artificial Intelligence (AI), Machine Learning (ML), Robotic Process Automation (RPA), Blockchain, and the Internet of Things (IoT), the institution embarked on a strategic digital transformation initiative.

Challenge

The institution faced several challenges, including legacy systems that hindered operational efficiency, increasing demand for personalized customer services, and the need for higher data security and transparency in transactions. Additionally, the competitive landscape required the institution to innovate continually to retain and attract customers.

Solution

AI and ML Integration: The institution integrated AI and ML algorithms to analyze customer data, enabling personalized financial advice and product offerings. This approach significantly improved customer satisfaction and engagement by delivering tailored experiences.

RPA Deployment: To enhance operational efficiency, RPA was deployed to automate repetitive and time-consuming tasks such as account opening processes, data entry, and compliance checks. This automation resulted in a reduction in processing times and operational costs while allowing employees to focus on higher-value tasks.

Blockchain for Secure Transactions: Recognizing the need for enhanced security and transparency, the institution implemented Blockchain technology for secure, transparent, and efficient transaction processing. This not only improved trust among customers but also streamlined cross-border transactions, reducing costs and settlement times.

IoT for Enhanced Services: The institution explored IoT technologies to develop innovative banking services, such as fraud detection systems that analyze customer behavior and transaction patterns in real-time. IoT devices were also used to enhance the in-branch customer experience, offering personalized services as soon as a customer entered the branch.

Conclusion

This case study demonstrates the transformative power of emerging technologies in the financial services sector. By strategically implementing AI, ML, RPA, Blockchain, and IoT, the institution not only overcame its operational and customer service challenges but also established itself as a leader in digital innovation. The success of this initiative highlights the importance of adopting a forward-thinking approach to technology, ensuring that financial institutions can meet evolving customer expectations and navigate the challenges of the digital age.

Below are the questions related to the above case study:

1. What were the main challenges faced by the financial institution before implementing emerging technologies?

2. Which emerging technologies did the financial institution implement to address its challenges?

3. How did AI and ML contribute to improving customer engagement and satisfaction?

4. What operational benefits did the institution experience from deploying RPA?

5. In what ways did Blockchain technology enhance transaction processing for the institution?

6. How did the institution use IoT technologies to improve services and security?

7. What was the overall impact of the digital transformation initiative on the institution's competitive position in the market?

Part II: Technologies Driving Change

Chapter 4: Artificial Intelligence in ITSM

Artificial Intelligence (AI) in IT Service Management (ITSM) represents a significant advancement in leveraging technology to enhance operational efficiency, improve service delivery, and optimize IT processes. AI in ITSM involves the use of AI-powered technologies such as machine learning, natural language processing, and predictive analytics to automate tasks, analyze data, and optimize IT service delivery.

Real-time case studies provide tangible examples of how AI is transforming ITSM practices. For instance, a global tech company implemented an AI-driven incident management system that analyzed historical incident data to predict and prevent future issues. This resulted in a 40% reduction in meantime to resolution (MTTR) and improved service uptime. In another example, a leading financial institution deployed AI-powered chatbots to handle customer inquiries and support requests. The chatbots provided instant assistance, reducing service desk inquiries by 30% and enhancing customer satisfaction.

The benefits of AI in ITSM extend to both business and IT users. Improved efficiency is one of the primary benefits, as AI automates repetitive tasks, accelerates incident resolution, and optimizes resource allocation. This leads to increased productivity and allows IT departments to focus on strategic initiatives. Additionally, AI-powered chatbots offer personalized interactions and 24/7 availability, improving the overall IT service experience for users and enhancing customer satisfaction. Furthermore, AI-driven predictive analytics enable organizations to identify and address potential IT issues before they impact operations, minimizing service disruptions and downtime.

AI helps IT departments become more efficient in several ways. Firstly, it automates routine tasks such as ticket categorization, prioritization, and assignment, freeing up human resources for more strategic initiatives. Predictive insights and analytics provided by AI enable IT departments to anticipate and address issues before they escalate, improving operational efficiency and reliability. Additionally, AI-powered chatbots offer personalized support and self-service options, empowering users to resolve issues independently and reducing the workload on IT support staff.

Applications and case studies

Artificial Intelligence (AI) has revolutionized IT Service Management (ITSM), offering innovative solutions to streamline processes, enhance efficiency, and improve customer experiences. In this chapter, we will explore various applications of AI in ITSM along with real-world case studies demonstrating its effectiveness.

Automated Incident Management:

AI-powered algorithms analyze historical incident data to predict and prevent future issues, leading to faster incident resolution and reduced downtime. A global technology company implemented an AI-driven incident management system that reduced mean time to resolution (MTTR) by 40%, resulting in improved service uptime and customer satisfaction.

Following is the incident management procedure:

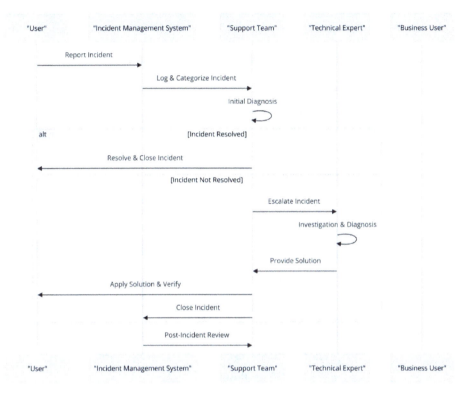

Incident Management, according to ITIL V3, aims to restore normal service operation as quickly as possible and minimize the adverse impact on business operations, thus ensuring that the best possible levels of service quality and availability are maintained.

Key Steps in the Incident Management Process:

1. **Incident Identification**: Detection and recording of an incident.

2. **Incident Logging**: All details of the incident are logged and documented.

3. **Incident Categorization**: Assigning a category to the incident for easier management and routing.

4. **Incident Prioritization**: Determining the urgency and impact to assign a priority for timely handling.

5. **Initial Diagnosis**: Attempting to resolve the incident with an immediate solution or workaround.

6. **Incident Escalation**: If not resolved at initial diagnosis, the incident may be escalated for further investigation.

   - **Functional Escalation**: If more expertise is needed.

   - **Hierarchical Escalation**: If high impact or urgency is detected.

7. **Investigation and Diagnosis**: Detailed analysis to identify the root cause.

8. **Resolution and Recovery**: Once a fix is found, it is applied to resolve the incident and restore service.

9. **Incident Closure**: After confirming resolution with the business user, the incident is formally closed.

10. **Post-Incident Review**: Reviewing and documenting lessons learned and improvements for future incidents.

Descriptions:

- **Incident Identification**: The trigger for the incident management process, identifying something is wrong either through automated alerts or user reports.

- **Incident Logging**: Every detail about the incident is recorded for accountability and future reference.

- **Incident Categorization**: Helps in organizing incidents into logical groups for better management.

- **Incident Prioritization**: Ensures that incidents with the highest impact and urgency are dealt with first.

- **Initial Diagnosis**: A quick fix or workaround to minimize the impact on the business.

- **Incident Escalation**: Escalation is necessary when the initial support tier cannot resolve the incident. Functional escalation is for technical expertise, while hierarchical escalation is for issues affecting critical business processes or needing management attention.

- **Investigation and Diagnosis**: In-depth analysis to find the root cause of the incident.

- **Resolution and Recovery**: Implementing a fix or workaround to restore service.

- **Incident Closure**: Formal closure of the incident after verification that the issue is resolved.

- **Post-Incident Review**: An essential step for continuous improvement, analyzing what was done well and what could be improved.

Intelligent Chatbots for Customer Support:

AI chatbots handle routine service requests, provide instant support, and guide users through troubleshooting processes, reducing service desk inquiries and improving response times. For example, a leading e-commerce platform deployed AI-powered chatbots on its website, resulting in a 30% reduction in service desk inquiries and enhanced customer satisfaction scores.

Predictive Analytics for Capacity Planning:

AI and machine learning algorithms forecast capacity requirements based on IT infrastructure data, optimizing resource allocation and improving performance. In a case study, a healthcare organization utilized AI-driven predictive analytics to accurately forecast server capacity needs, resulting in cost savings and improved scalability.

Automated Service Desk Operations:

AI automates repetitive service desk tasks such as ticket categorization, prioritization, and assignment, reducing manual effort and accelerating incident resolution. A financial institution implemented an AI-powered service desk solution that reduced manual ticket handling efforts by 50%, allowing service desk agents to focus on more complex issues.

Proactive Problem Management with AI Insights:

AI-driven analytics provide insights into potential IT issues before they escalate, enabling proactive problem management and minimizing service disruptions. For instance, a telecommunications company leveraged AI-driven insights to proactively identify network anomalies and address underlying issues, resulting in improved system reliability and reduced downtime.

Continuous Improvement through AI-Driven Feedback Analysis:

AI analyzes user feedback and service evaluations to identify areas for improvement and prioritize enhancement initiatives, fostering a culture of continuous improvement. A software development firm integrated AI-driven feedback analysis into its ITSM processes, resulting in higher customer satisfaction and improved service quality over time.

Conclusion:

AI has transformed ITSM practices by automating tasks, providing predictive insights, and enhancing the overall service experience for users. The real-world case studies presented in this chapter demonstrate the tangible benefits of AI in optimizing ITSM processes, increasing efficiency, and delivering greater value to organizations. As AI technologies continue to evolve, they will play an increasingly pivotal role in shaping the future of ITSM and driving innovation in the digital era.

Integrating AI with existing IT infrastructure

Integrating Artificial Intelligence (AI) with existing IT infrastructure is a crucial aspect of leveraging AI for IT Service Management (ITSM). This chapter explores the challenges, strategies, and benefits associated with integrating AI into established ITSM frameworks and infrastructure.

Integrating AI with existing IT infrastructure requires careful planning and consideration of various factors. One challenge is ensuring compatibility between AI systems and legacy ITSM tools and platforms. Legacy systems may have limitations in terms of data accessibility, interoperability, and scalability, which must be addressed to enable seamless integration with AI technologies. Additionally, organizations need to assess their data readiness, ensuring that they have clean, standardized data available for AI analysis and modeling.

A key strategy for integrating AI with existing IT infrastructure is through the use of application programming interfaces (APIs) and middleware solutions. APIs facilitate communication and data exchange between AI systems and existing ITSM platforms, enabling seamless integration without disrupting workflows or existing processes. Middleware solutions act as intermediaries, translating data formats and protocols to enable interoperability between AI and ITSM systems.

Another approach to integrating AI with existing IT infrastructure is through phased implementation and iterative development. Rather than attempting to overhaul the entire ITSM framework at once, organizations can start with pilot projects or proof-of-concepts to demonstrate the value of AI and validate its feasibility within their existing infrastructure. This incremental approach allows organizations to address challenges and refine their integration strategy based on real-world feedback and experiences.

The benefits of integrating AI with existing IT infrastructure in ITSM are numerous. AI-powered systems can automate routine tasks, analyze large volumes of data, and provide predictive insights, leading to improved efficiency, accuracy, and decision-making. For example, AI-driven analytics can help identify patterns and trends in ITSM data, enabling organizations to proactively detect and resolve issues before they impact operations. Additionally, AI-powered chatbots can enhance user experiences by providing instant support and personalized assistance, reducing service desk inquiries and improving customer satisfaction.

Furthermore, integrating AI with existing IT infrastructure enables organizations to future-proof their ITSM frameworks and prepare for emerging technologies and trends. By leveraging AI, organizations can stay ahead of the curve and adapt to changing business requirements and technological advancements. This flexibility and agility are essential for maintaining competitiveness and driving innovation in today's rapidly evolving digital landscape.

In conclusion, integrating AI with existing IT infrastructure in ITSM is a complex yet rewarding endeavor. By overcoming challenges and adopting effective strategies, organizations can harness the power of AI to optimize ITSM processes, enhance user experiences, and achieve business objectives. As AI technologies continue to evolve, organizations must remain proactive in their approach to integration, ensuring that AI complements and enhances existing IT infrastructure to drive value and innovation.

Questions and Answers

Q1. How can we assess the readiness of our existing IT infrastructure for integrating AI technologies into our ITSM framework?

Answer: Assessing the readiness of our existing IT infrastructure involves evaluating factors such as compatibility with AI systems, data accessibility, interoperability, scalability, and the cultural readiness of our IT staff. Conducting a comprehensive assessment will help identify any potential barriers or limitations that need to be addressed before integrating AI technologies into our ITSM framework.

Q2. What are the potential challenges and risks associated with integrating AI with our existing IT infrastructure, and how can we mitigate them?

Answer: Potential challenges and risks associated with integrating AI with our existing IT infrastructure include compatibility issues with legacy systems, data fragmentation, resistance to change among staff, concerns about data security and privacy, and resource constraints. These challenges can be mitigated through careful planning, investment in staff training and change management initiatives, implementation of robust data governance and security measures, and collaboration with ITSM vendors and AI solution providers.

Q3. What strategies can we employ to ensure seamless interoperability between AI systems and our legacy ITSM platforms?

Answer: Strategies to ensure seamless interoperability between AI systems and legacy ITSM platforms include leveraging middleware solutions, APIs, and integration tools to facilitate communication and data exchange. Collaborating closely with ITSM vendors and AI solution providers can also help ensure compatibility and interoperability between systems.

Q4. How can we prioritize AI integration initiatives within our IT department, considering competing demands and resource constraints?

Answer: Prioritizing AI integration initiatives within our IT department involves evaluating the potential impact and ROI of each initiative, considering factors such as cost, complexity, and alignment with strategic objectives. Conducting a cost-benefit analysis can help identify high-priority projects that deliver maximum value and address critical business needs. Resources and manpower should be allocated accordingly to ensure successful implementation and adoption.

Q5. What are the key performance indicators (KPIs) we should track to measure the success and impact of AI integration on our ITSM processes?

Answer: Key performance indicators (KPIs) to track the success and impact of AI integration on our ITSM processes may include metrics such as incident resolution time, service uptime, customer satisfaction scores, and cost savings. Monitoring these KPIs regularly allows us to assess the effectiveness of AI-driven initiatives, identify areas for improvement, and make data-driven decisions to optimize ITSM performance.

Q6. What are the potential benefits of integrating AI with our existing IT infrastructure in terms of improving operational efficiency, service quality, and customer satisfaction?

Answer: The potential benefits of integrating AI with our existing IT infrastructure include improved operational efficiency, enhanced service quality, and increased customer satisfaction. AI-powered automation streamlines ITSM processes, reducing manual effort and accelerating incident resolution. Predictive analytics enable proactive problem management, minimizing service disruptions and optimizing IT operations. AI-powered chatbots enhance user experiences by providing instant support and personalized assistance, leading to higher customer satisfaction scores.

Q7. How can we justify the investment in AI integration to senior management and stakeholders, demonstrating the potential return on investment (ROI) and long-term value?

Answer: Justifying the investment in AI integration to senior management and stakeholders involves demonstrating the potential return on investment (ROI) and long-term value through a compelling business case. This includes outlining the expected benefits, cost savings, and strategic advantages of AI integration, backed by concrete data and evidence. Presenting a clear roadmap for implementation and adoption, along with projected ROI calculations, can help build confidence and support for the investment.

Q8. What are the best practices for selecting and implementing AI technologies that align with our organization's ITSM objectives and business goals?

Answer: Best practices for selecting and implementing AI technologies include conducting thorough research and evaluation of available options, assessing compatibility with ITSM objectives and business goals, piloting solutions to test feasibility and effectiveness, and involving key stakeholders in the decision-making process. Additionally, collaborating with reputable vendors and seeking recommendations from industry experts can help ensure that selected AI technologies align with our organization's specific needs and requirements.

Q9. How can we ensure data security and privacy when integrating AI with our existing IT infrastructure, especially considering sensitive information handled within ITSM processes?

Answer: Ensuring data security and privacy when integrating AI with our existing IT infrastructure involves implementing robust data governance and security measures. This includes encryption of sensitive data, access controls, monitoring and auditing mechanisms, compliance with regulations such as GDPR and CCPA, and regular security assessments and updates. Additionally, staff training and awareness programs can help promote a culture of data security and privacy awareness throughout the organization.

Q10. What role does organizational culture and change management play in successfully integrating AI with our existing IT infrastructure, and how can we promote adoption and acceptance among IT staff?

Answer: Organizational culture and change management play a critical role in successfully integrating AI with existing IT infrastructure. Promoting adoption and acceptance among IT staff requires effective communication, training, and support initiatives to address concerns, build confidence, and foster a culture of innovation and collaboration. Involving IT staff in the integration process, providing opportunities for skill development and upskilling, and recognizing and rewarding contributions can help promote a positive and receptive attitude towards AI technologies.

Case Study: Artificial Intelligence in IT Service Management (ITSM)

Company Background: MicroByte Innovations is a multinational technology company providing a range of IT services to clients across various industries. With a large and complex IT infrastructure supporting its operations, MicroByte Innovations faces challenges in efficiently managing IT services, addressing incidents, and meeting customer demands.

Integration of Artificial Intelligence: In response to these challenges, MicroByte Innovations decides to integrate artificial intelligence (AI) into its ITSM framework. The company implements AI-powered solutions across various ITSM processes, including incident management, service desk operations, and change management.

Applications and Benefits:

1. Incident Management: MicroByte Innovations deploys AI-driven algorithms to analyze historical incident data and identify patterns and trends. This enables proactive incident resolution by predicting potential issues before they occur, minimizing service disruptions, and reducing downtime.

2. Service Desk Operations: AI-powered chatbots are implemented to provide instant support and assistance to users. These chatbots leverage natural language processing (NLP) and machine learning algorithms to understand user queries, troubleshoot issues, and provide relevant solutions. This improves response times, enhances user experiences, and reduces the workload on service desk agents.

3. Change Management: AI is used to automate routine change management tasks, such as impact analysis and risk assessment. By analyzing historical change data and identifying potential risks, AI helps expedite the change approval process while ensuring compliance with organizational policies and regulatory requirements.

4. Predictive Analytics: MicroByte Innovations utilizes AI-powered predictive analytics to forecast future ITSM trends, identify areas for process optimization, and make data-driven decisions. By analyzing large volumes of historical data, AI generates insights that help optimize resource allocation, improve service quality, and drive continuous improvement initiatives.

Questions:

1. How did MicroByte Innovations decide to integrate artificial intelligence into its ITSM framework?

2. What specific challenges and pain points prompted MicroByte Innovations to explore AI-powered solutions for ITSM?

3. Can you explain how MicroByte Innovations utilized AI in incident management and the benefits it achieved?

4. How did AI-powered chatbots enhance service desk operations at MicroByte Innovations?

5. What role did AI play in change management processes at MicroByte Innovations, and how did it impact efficiency and compliance?

6. Can you elaborate on the use of predictive analytics powered by AI at MicroByte Innovations and its impact on ITSM decision-making?

7. What were the key considerations and challenges MicroByte Innovations faced during the integration of AI into its ITSM framework?

8. How did MicroByte Innovations ensure data security and privacy when implementing AI-powered solutions in ITSM?

9. What were the outcomes and measurable benefits achieved by MicroByte Innovations after integrating AI into its ITSM processes?

10. How did the organizational culture at MicroByte Innovations contribute to the successful adoption and implementation of AI in ITSM?

Chapter 5: The Impact of Automation and RPA

In the rapidly evolving landscape of Information Technology Service Management (ITSM), the role of automation and Robotic Process Automation (RPA) has surged to the forefront, catalyzing a significant transformation in operational procedures, efficiency, and accuracy. The advent of these technologies has not merely altered the operational paradigms but has set new standards for service delivery within ITSM frameworks. This chapter explores the profound implications of integrating automation and RPA into ITSM, emphasizing their contributions to streamlining operations and bolstering both efficiency and accuracy.

Automation and RPA have introduced a level of operational fluidity that was previously unattainable, significantly streamlining ITSM processes. For instance, the automation of incident and request management systems enables the handling, categorization, and routing of service requests and incidents with minimal human intervention. This not only expedites the resolution process but also allows IT personnel to dedicate their focus to more complex issues, thereby enhancing the overall service experience. Additionally, the optimization of workflow management through automation eradicates manual, time-consuming tasks, further refined by RPA's capacity to mimic human actions, ensuring swift, seamless operations devoid of bottlenecks. Furthermore, automation facilitates proactive problem management by identifying potential issues before they escalate, thereby reducing downtime and augmenting system reliability.

The efficiency and accuracy enhancements attributable to automation and RPA within ITSM are substantial. Operational efficiency sees a marked increase as automation reduces the need for manual interventions in routine tasks, consequently minimizing delays. RPA amplifies this efficiency by executing tasks continuously, optimizing IT services without the need for additional human resources. Moreover, the reduction in human errors due to predefined rules and parameters in automated tasks significantly boosts operational and reporting accuracy. Compliance and governance also benefit, as automation tools adhere to established standards and policies, simplifying compliance management. Lastly, the optimal allocation of human resources towards strategic and core activities fosters innovation and strategic growth, further emphasizing the value added by automation and RPA.

Despite the numerous benefits, the implementation of automation and RPA is not devoid of challenges. Considerations such as the initial setup and integration costs, the necessity for continuous maintenance and updates, and the potential for job displacement necessitate a strategic approach. This approach should focus on complementing rather than replacing human efforts, ensuring a balanced integration of automation technologies within ITSM processes.

The integration of automation and Robotic Process Automation (RPA) into IT Service Management (ITSM) significantly streamlines operations, enhancing both efficiency and accuracy within the IT services sector. These technological advancements have been instrumental in transforming the landscape of IT operations, setting new benchmarks for service delivery that prioritize speed, precision, and reliability.

Streamlining Operations through Automation and RPA

The essence of streamlining operations in ITSM lies in the automation of routine and repetitive tasks, which traditionally consumed a significant amount of time and resources. Automation tools and RPA bots are designed to handle such tasks with unparalleled speed and consistency. For example, automated incident and request management systems can capture, categorize, and route service requests and incidents without human intervention, significantly reducing response times and increasing throughput. This level of automation ensures that IT professionals can allocate more time to tackle complex issues and strategic initiatives, thereby enhancing the service experience for end-users.

Moreover, automation in ITSM extends to optimizing workflow management. It eliminates manual bottlenecks, ensuring that processes are executed swiftly and seamlessly. RPA, with its ability to replicate human actions, further streamlines these workflows, enabling operations that run more efficiently. By automating scheduled maintenance and updates, IT services can operate on the latest software versions with minimal downtime, contributing to a more reliable IT infrastructure.

Enhancing Efficiency and Accuracy

The deployment of automation and RPA in ITSM goes beyond just operational streamlining; it significantly boosts both efficiency and accuracy across IT operations. By automating tasks, organizations can achieve a higher operational tempo and reduce the likelihood of delays caused by manual processes. RPA enhances this effect by offering 24/7 operational capabilities without the need for rest, ensuring that IT services are continuously optimized.

One of the most notable benefits of automation is the reduction in human errors. Automated processes follow precise instructions, minimizing the risk of mistakes that can occur with manual intervention. This increase in accuracy is critical for maintaining high standards of service delivery and reliability. Furthermore, automation aids in achieving improved compliance and governance by ensuring that all operations adhere to predefined standards and policies, thereby facilitating easier management and auditability.

Automation and RPA also contribute to optimized resource allocation. By freeing up IT professionals from mundane tasks, resources can be redirected towards areas that contribute more significantly to business value, such as innovation and strategic projects. This shift not only enhances the efficiency of the IT department but also drives overall business growth.

Conclusion

The impact of automation and RPA on streamlining operations and enhancing efficiency and accuracy in ITSM is profound. These technologies offer a pathway to operational excellence, enabling IT services to be more agile, responsive, and efficient. As the digital landscape continues to evolve, the strategic implementation of automation and RPA will be crucial for organizations aiming to stay ahead in the competitive IT services market. By embracing these advancements, ITSM can significantly improve service delivery, operational reliability, and customer satisfaction, marking a significant leap forward in the pursuit of technological and operational excellence.

Questions and Answers

Q1: How do automation and RPA streamline operations in IT Service Management (ITSM)?

A1: Automation and RPA streamline operations in ITSM by automating routine and repetitive tasks, such as incident and request management, workflow optimization, and scheduled maintenance. This reduces manual intervention, speeds up processes, and ensures that IT professionals can focus on more complex issues and strategic initiatives.

Q2: What role does RPA play in enhancing the efficiency of ITSM processes?

A2: RPA enhances the efficiency of ITSM processes by executing tasks 24/7 without the need for rest, thereby optimizing IT services continuously. It replicates human actions to perform tasks swiftly and accurately, enabling operations to run more efficiently and without manual bottlenecks.

Q3: How does automation contribute to the accuracy of ITSM operations?

A3: Automation contributes to the accuracy of ITSM operations by minimizing human errors. Automated tasks follow precise, predefined instructions, reducing the risk of mistakes associated with manual processes. This ensures high standards of service delivery and reliability.

Q4: In what ways does automation and RPA impact compliance and governance within ITSM?

A4: Automation and RPA positively impact compliance and governance within ITSM by ensuring that operations adhere to predefined standards and policies. This facilitates easier management and auditability, as automated processes are designed to comply with regulatory frameworks, enhancing overall governance.

Q5: How does the implementation of automation and RPA affect resource allocation in IT departments? A5: The implementation of automation and RPA affects resource allocation by freeing up IT professionals from mundane tasks, allowing them to focus on areas that add more significant business value, such as innovation and strategic projects. This optimized allocation of resources not only improves the efficiency of the IT department but also drives business growth.

Q6: What are the key benefits of integrating automation and RPA into ITSM?

A6: The key benefits of integrating automation and RPA into ITSM include streamlined operations, enhanced efficiency, reduced human errors, improved compliance and governance, and optimized resource allocation. These benefits contribute to operational excellence, enabling more agile, responsive, and efficient IT services.

Q7: Can you describe a scenario where RPA significantly improved an ITSM process?

A7: A scenario where RPA significantly improved an ITSM process involves the automated handling of service requests and incidents. RPA bots were programmed to categorize and route incoming tickets automatically, reducing response times by a significant margin and allowing IT staff to concentrate on resolving more complex issues, thereby improving the overall service experience.

Case Study: Automation and RPA Transformation in Global IT Services

Background

A leading global IT services company faced challenges in managing its growing volume of service requests and incidents. The manual handling of these tasks led to increased response times, higher error rates, and inconsistent service quality. The company recognized the need to streamline operations and enhance efficiency and accuracy to maintain its competitive edge and ensure customer satisfaction.

Solution Implementation

The company decided to implement automation and RPA technologies within its IT Service Management (ITSM) framework. The initiative focused on two main areas:

1. **Automated Incident and Request Management:** The company introduced an automation platform to handle incoming service requests and incidents automatically. This system was capable of categorizing, prioritizing, and routing tickets to the appropriate teams without human intervention.

2. **RPA for Routine IT Tasks:** RPA bots were deployed to perform routine IT tasks, such as password resets, system monitoring, and regular maintenance checks. These bots were designed to operate 24/7, ensuring continuous service optimization.

Results

The implementation of automation and RPA led to significant improvements in the company's ITSM processes:

- **Reduced Response Times:** Automated ticketing and routing reduced the average response time by 40%, enhancing the overall service experience for end-users.

- **Increased Accuracy:** The error rate in incident handling and routine IT tasks decreased by 50% due to the precision of automation and RPA.

- **Higher Efficiency:** The IT team's productivity increased as they could focus on more complex and strategic tasks, with routine operations being managed by RPA bots.

- **Improved Customer Satisfaction:** The streamlined operations and improved service quality led to a 30% increase in customer satisfaction scores.

Conclusion

The company's strategic implementation of automation and RPA transformed its ITSM operations, demonstrating the powerful impact of these technologies on streamlining operations and enhancing efficiency and accuracy. This case study serves as a testament to the potential of automation and RPA in revolutionizing IT service management.

Questions for Case Study Discussion

Q1: What were the main challenges faced by the IT services company before implementing automation and RPA?

Q2: How did automated incident and request management contribute to reduced response times?

Q3: In what ways did RPA bots improve the efficiency and accuracy of routine IT tasks?

Q4: Discuss the impact of automation and RPA on the productivity of the IT team and overall customer satisfaction.

Q5: What lessons can be learned from this case study about the implementation of automation and RPA in ITSM processes?

Chapter 6: Embracing General AI and Advanced Analytics

Introduction

The integration of Artificial Intelligence (AI) and Advanced Analytics into the fabric of IT Service Management (ITSM) heralds a new era in the way IT services are conceptualized, delivered, and managed. This transformative journey towards a more predictive, intelligent, and efficient ITSM landscape is underpinned by the advancements in General AI and Predictive Analytics. This chapter seeks to explore the profound implications of these technologies on ITSM, delineating their roles in enhancing predictive capabilities and unlocking the vast potential of AI-driven service management.

The Advent of Predictive Analytics in ITSM

Predictive Analytics represents a pivotal shift in ITSM, moving from traditional reactive models to a more proactive, data-driven approach. This section delves into the core aspects of Predictive Analytics within ITSM, illustrating its impact on various operational dimensions.

Enhancing Incident Prediction Predictive Analytics empowers ITSM teams with the foresight to anticipate and mitigate incidents before they escalate into significant disruptions. By analyzing historical data, these advanced analytics tools identify patterns and trends, offering predictions on potential future incidents. This predictive capability enables ITSM professionals to implement preemptive measures, ensuring a robust, uninterrupted business operation.

Optimizing Capacity Planning The strategic application of Predictive Analytics extends to capacity planning, where it plays a crucial role in forecasting the demand for IT resources. By accurately predicting future needs, ITSM can ensure that the IT infrastructure is precisely aligned with business demands, thereby optimizing resource utilization and avoiding both overprovisioning and underutilization.

Driving Continuous Service Improvement Predictive Analytics also serves as a cornerstone for continuous service improvement initiatives. By analyzing data from customer feedback, service usage patterns, and performance metrics, ITSM teams can uncover actionable insights for service enhancements. This ongoing optimization process is rooted in actual user needs and behaviors, ensuring that IT services evolve in alignment with customer expectations.

Unveiling the Future Potentials of General AI in ITSM

Artificial General Intelligence (AGI) represents the zenith of AI development, where AI systems exhibit human-like intelligence across a broad spectrum of cognitive tasks. The prospective integration of AGI into ITSM opens up a realm of possibilities for redefining service delivery and management.

Realizing Autonomous IT Operations The advent of AGI promises a future where IT operations achieve a level of autonomy previously unimaginable. In this scenario, AGI systems would autonomously manage and optimize IT infrastructure, performing tasks such as incident resolution, system optimization, and predictive resource allocation without human intervention. This autonomous operational model signifies a monumental leap towards achieving maximum operational efficiency and reliability.

Facilitating Enhanced Decision Making AGI's unparalleled data processing and analytical capabilities could revolutionize decision-making processes within ITSM. By synthesizing insights from vast datasets, AGI could provide ITSM professionals with deep, actionable intelligence, thereby significantly enhancing strategic planning and operational decision-making.

Personalizing the User Experience AGI holds the potential to dramatically personalize IT service delivery, tailoring services to meet individual user preferences, behaviors, and requirements. This level of personalization could transform the user experience, fostering higher levels of satisfaction and productivity.

Spurring Innovation and New Service Development The capabilities of AGI may also catalyze the creation of innovative IT services and solutions, pushing the boundaries of current technology and offering new avenues for business growth and competitive differentiation.

Navigating Challenges and Ethical Considerations

The journey towards integrating General AI and advanced analytics into ITSM is fraught with challenges and ethical considerations. Issues surrounding data privacy, security, and the ethical deployment of AI technologies must be meticulously navigated to fully realize the benefits of these advancements in a responsible and sustainable manner.

Conclusion

The integration of General AI and advanced analytics heralds a transformative era for ITSM, characterized by predictive capabilities, enhanced efficiency, and a new level of service personalization. As these technologies continue to evolve, their strategic implementation will be critical for organizations seeking to redefine the landscape of IT service delivery and management. This chapter has laid the groundwork for understanding the profound impact of these technologies on

ITSM, setting the stage for a future where IT services are not only more intelligent and efficient but also more aligned with the dynamic needs of businesses and end-users.

Questions and Answers

Q1: What role does Predictive Analytics play in transforming IT Service Management (ITSM)? A1: Predictive Analytics transforms ITSM by enabling a shift from reactive to proactive management. It enhances incident prediction, optimizes capacity planning, and drives continuous service improvement through data analysis. This results in reduced downtime, better resource utilization, and services that evolve according to user needs.

Q2: How does Predictive Analytics improve incident management within ITSM? A2: Predictive Analytics improves incident management by analyzing historical data to identify patterns and trends that predict future incidents. This allows ITSM teams to take preemptive actions to mitigate potential issues before they impact business operations, enhancing operational reliability and continuity.

Q3: What is the significance of Artificial General Intelligence (AGI) in the future of ITSM? A3: AGI signifies the pinnacle of AI development, offering the potential for ITSM operations to achieve unprecedented levels of autonomy, intelligence, and efficiency. AGI could autonomously manage IT infrastructure, enhance decision-making with deep insights, personalize user experiences, and drive innovation in IT service development.

Q4: Can you describe how AGI might achieve autonomous IT operations? A4: AGI could achieve autonomous IT operations by independently performing tasks such as incident resolution, system optimization, and predictive resource allocation. This autonomy is based on AGI's ability to understand, learn, and apply intelligence across various tasks, minimizing the need for human intervention and maximizing operational efficiency.

Q5: What challenges and ethical considerations must be addressed when integrating General AI and advanced analytics into ITSM? A5: Integrating General AI and advanced analytics into ITSM raises several challenges and ethical considerations, including data privacy, security, and the responsible use of AI technologies. Addressing these concerns involves ensuring transparency, accountability, and adherence to ethical guidelines to responsibly harness the benefits of these advancements.

Q6: How does Predictive Analytics contribute to capacity planning in ITSM? A6: Predictive Analytics contributes to capacity planning by forecasting future demand for IT resources, enabling ITSM teams to adjust their infrastructure accordingly. This predictive capability ensures that resources are allocated efficiently, avoiding overprovisioning and resource shortages, and aligning IT capabilities with business needs.

Q7: In what ways could AGI personalize IT service delivery? A7: AGI could personalize IT service delivery by analyzing individual user preferences, behaviors, and requirements to tailor services accordingly. This level of personalization would enhance user satisfaction and productivity by providing services that are specifically designed to meet the unique needs of each user.

Case Study: Revolutionizing ITSM with Predictive Analytics and AGI at TechGlobal Inc.

Background

TechGlobal Inc., a leading multinational corporation, faced significant challenges in managing its IT services due to increasing service requests, incidents, and the complexity of its IT infrastructure. The company recognized the need to transition from a reactive ITSM model to a more proactive, data-driven approach.

Implementation

To address these challenges, TechGlobal Inc. embarked on a transformative journey by integrating Predictive Analytics and exploring the potential of Artificial General Intelligence (AGI) within its ITSM framework.

Predictive Analytics for Incident Management: TechGlobal Inc. implemented Predictive Analytics to analyze historical incident data, enabling the ITSM team to identify patterns and predict potential future incidents. This allowed for preemptive actions to mitigate or entirely avoid these incidents, significantly reducing downtime and improving system reliability.

Capacity Planning with Advanced Analytics: The company utilized Advanced Analytics for dynamic capacity planning, accurately forecasting the demand for IT resources. This ensured optimal resource allocation, preventing both resource shortages and overprovisioning, thereby aligning IT capabilities with business needs more effectively.

Exploring AGI for Autonomous Operations: TechGlobal Inc. initiated a pilot project to explore the use of AGI in automating routine IT tasks and decision-making processes. The goal was to achieve a level of IT operations autonomy previously unattainable, aiming for systems that could self-optimize and resolve incidents independently.

Results

The integration of Predictive Analytics and the exploration of AGI brought about remarkable improvements in TechGlobal Inc.'s ITSM operations:

- **Reduced Incidents and Downtime:** The predictive capabilities led to a 40% reduction in critical incidents, significantly enhancing system uptime and reliability.

- **Efficient Resource Utilization:** Advanced capacity planning resulted in a 30% improvement in resource utilization, reducing costs and enhancing service delivery.

- **Pioneering Autonomous IT Operations:** Although still in the early stages, the AGI pilot project demonstrated potential for further reducing manual interventions and improving operational efficiency.

Conclusion

TechGlobal Inc.'s initiative to embrace Predictive Analytics and AGI within its ITSM operations exemplifies a forward-thinking approach to managing IT services. By transitioning to a more proactive and autonomous ITSM model, the company has set a benchmark for innovation in IT service management.

Questions for Case Study Discussion

Q1: How did Predictive Analytics help TechGlobal Inc. in reducing incidents and improving system reliability?

Q2: In what ways did Advanced Analytics impact capacity planning at TechGlobal Inc.?

Q3: What potential benefits does AGI offer to autonomous IT operations, based on TechGlobal Inc.'s pilot project?

Q4: Discuss the challenges TechGlobal Inc. might face in fully integrating AGI into its ITSM operations.

Q5: How can TechGlobal Inc. ensure ethical considerations are addressed while implementing AGI and Advanced Analytics in ITSM?

Chapter 7: Governance Strategies for a Digital World

Introduction

In the digital era, where technology drives innovation and growth, the strategic alignment of IT governance with corporate strategy has become a pivotal element of organizational success. As businesses navigate through the complexities of digital transformation, the need for robust governance strategies that can adapt to the rapid pace of technological change is more critical than ever. This chapter explores the multifaceted approach to governance in the digital age, emphasizing the importance of strategic management, cybersecurity, and risk management.

The Imperative of Strategic Alignment

The convergence of IT and business strategies is essential for organizations aiming to leverage digital technologies for competitive advantage. The alignment ensures that IT investments and initiatives are in direct correlation with the business's strategic objectives, facilitating innovation, efficiency, and market responsiveness.

Strategic Planning and Collaboration

Strategic alignment begins with an integrated planning process that involves IT and business leaders working collaboratively to define a unified vision. This collaborative approach ensures that IT initiatives are not just supportive of but are integral to the achievement of business goals. For instance, a retail company might integrate e-commerce platforms directly into its sales strategy to enhance customer experience and drive sales.

Frameworks for Alignment

Frameworks such as COBIT (Control Objectives for Information and Related Technologies) and ITIL (Information Technology Infrastructure Library) provide structured approaches to managing IT processes, ensuring they align with business strategies. These frameworks facilitate a common language and understanding between IT and business leaders, promoting effective communication and collaboration.

Agile Governance

In the fast-paced digital environment, agility in governance allows organizations to adapt quickly to market changes and emerging technologies. Agile governance involves a flexible approach to decision-making and project management, focusing on iterative progress, feedback loops, and continuous improvement. This agility enables organizations to pivot strategies as needed, ensuring sustained alignment with business objectives.

Cybersecurity and Risk Management

As digital technologies become increasingly integrated into every aspect of business operations, the importance of cybersecurity and risk management has surged. Protecting digital assets, customer data, and proprietary information is paramount to maintaining trust and operational continuity.

Comprehensive Risk Management

Effective risk management in the digital age involves identifying, assessing, and mitigating risks associated with digital operations. This includes not only cybersecurity threats but also compliance risks, operational risks, and reputational risks. For example, the implementation of GDPR (General Data Protection Regulation) in Europe necessitated organizations worldwide to reassess their data handling and privacy policies, integrating compliance risk management into their overall digital strategy.

Cybersecurity Frameworks

Adopting cybersecurity frameworks such as the NIST Cybersecurity Framework helps organizations in managing and mitigating cybersecurity risks effectively. These frameworks provide guidelines for protecting information systems against threats, detecting security incidents, and responding to and recovering from cyber-attacks. Implementing such frameworks is crucial for establishing a resilient cybersecurity posture that supports the organization's strategic objectives.

Incident Response and Recovery

An effective incident response plan is a critical component of cybersecurity and risk management. Organizations must be prepared to respond swiftly and efficiently to security incidents to minimize their impact. This includes having a dedicated incident response team, clear communication channels, and predefined recovery processes. Continuous improvement through lessons learned from incidents is also vital for enhancing future resilience.

Cultivating a Digital Governance Culture

The success of governance strategies in a digital world also depends on the organizational culture. Cultivating a culture that embraces digital transformation, values cybersecurity, and understands the strategic importance of IT is essential.

Leadership and Vision

Leadership plays a crucial role in shaping the digital governance culture. Leaders must champion digital initiatives, demonstrate a commitment to cybersecurity, and foster an environment where innovation is encouraged, and risks are managed prudently.

Education and Awareness

Ongoing education and awareness programs for employees about the importance of cybersecurity, data protection, and adherence to governance policies are crucial. Empowering employees with the knowledge and tools to recognize and respond to cyber threats can significantly enhance the organization's security posture.

Collaboration and Engagement

Promoting collaboration and engagement across departments can help in breaking down silos and ensuring a unified approach to digital governance. Regular interactions, workshops, and cross-functional teams can facilitate the sharing of insights and best practices, strengthening the governance framework.

Navigating the Future of Digital Governance

As digital technologies continue to evolve, so too must the governance strategies that guide their use. Organizations must remain vigilant, adaptable, and forward-thinking to navigate the challenges and opportunities of the digital age.

Emerging Technologies and Governance

The advent of emerging technologies such as artificial intelligence (AI), blockchain, and the Internet of Things (IoT) presents new governance challenges and opportunities. Organizations must assess the implications of these technologies on their governance frameworks, considering aspects such as ethical use, data security, and regulatory compliance.

Global Trends and Compliance

Global trends, such as increasing regulatory requirements and the globalization of business operations, also influence digital governance strategies. Staying informed about these trends and adapting governance practices accordingly is essential for ensuring compliance and maintaining a competitive edge.

Aligning IT governance with corporate strategy

Aligning IT governance with corporate strategy is a crucial aspect of ensuring that an organization's IT investments and initiatives support its overarching business goals and objectives. This alignment ensures that IT resources are utilized effectively, risks are managed appropriately, and IT delivers value to the business. In this section, we will explore the importance of this alignment, strategies for achieving it, and recent scenarios that highlight its significance in the modern business landscape.

The Importance of Alignment

In today's digital economy, technology is a key driver of innovation, efficiency, and competitive advantage. As such, IT governance – the framework that guides how IT decisions are made and executed – must be closely aligned with the corporate strategy. This alignment ensures that:

- **IT Investments Support Business Goals:** Every IT project or initiative should directly contribute to the strategic objectives of the organization, whether it's entering new markets, enhancing customer experience, or improving operational efficiency.

- **Risk Management is Integrated:** The risks associated with IT, including cybersecurity threats and compliance issues, are aligned with the organization's risk management strategies, ensuring that they are identified, assessed, and mitigated in the context of business priorities.

- **Value Delivery is Optimized:** By aligning IT governance with corporate strategy, organizations can ensure that IT delivers maximum value, optimizing the return on technology investments and driving business growth.

Strategies for Achieving Alignment

Achieving alignment between IT governance and corporate strategy requires a concerted effort across several dimensions:

1. **Strategic Planning Integration:** IT strategic planning should be an integral part of the corporate strategic planning process. This involves IT leaders working closely with business executives to understand strategic goals and ensuring that IT strategies are developed to support these goals.

2. **Establishing a Governance Framework:** A robust IT governance framework that outlines the decision-making processes, roles, and responsibilities is essential. This framework should ensure that IT decisions are made in the context of business objectives and that there is clear accountability for outcomes.

3. **Communication and Collaboration:** Regular communication and collaboration between IT and business leaders are crucial for maintaining alignment. This can involve joint strategy sessions, regular update meetings, and cross-functional teams working on strategic initiatives.

4. **Performance Measurement:** Establishing key performance indicators (KPIs) that reflect both IT and business objectives is vital. These metrics should measure the impact of IT initiatives on business outcomes, ensuring that IT governance is driving the desired strategic results.

Latest Scenarios Illustrating the Importance of Alignment

Scenario 1: Digital Transformation in Retail A global retail chain embarked on a digital transformation initiative to enhance customer experience and streamline operations. By aligning its IT governance with the corporate strategy of becoming a customer-centric organization, the company implemented omnichannel retailing, personalized marketing, and efficient supply chain management systems. This alignment ensured that IT investments directly contributed to enhancing customer satisfaction and operational efficiency, driving significant growth in sales and market share.

Scenario 2: Cybersecurity and Risk Management in Finance A financial services firm faced increasing cybersecurity threats that posed significant risks to its operations and customer trust. By integrating its IT governance with the corporate strategy focused on trust and reliability, the firm prioritized investments in advanced cybersecurity technologies and compliance management systems. This alignment ensured that IT risk management was a core component of the firm's strategic approach to maintaining customer trust and adhering to regulatory requirements.

Scenario 3: Innovation and Competitive Advantage in Manufacturing A manufacturing company looking to gain a competitive edge through innovation aligned its IT governance with its corporate strategy of leveraging technology for innovation. The company invested in Internet of Things (IoT) technologies and advanced analytics to optimize its manufacturing processes and develop new, data-driven products. This strategic alignment enabled the company to not only improve operational efficiency but also create new revenue streams through innovative products.

Cybersecurity and risk management

Cybersecurity and risk management are critical components of modern business strategy, given the increasing prevalence of digital threats and the integral role of technology in business operations. This section explores the significance of integrating cybersecurity measures and risk management strategies into organizational practices, offering insights into effective frameworks and real-world scenarios that underscore the importance of a proactive stance on cybersecurity.

Understanding Cybersecurity and Risk Management

Cybersecurity involves protecting IT systems, networks, and data from cyber threats such as malware, ransomware, phishing, and data breaches. Risk management complements cybersecurity by identifying, assessing, and mitigating risks associated with these threats. Together, they form a defensive shield that safeguards an organization's information assets and ensures business continuity.

The Evolving Threat Landscape

The digital threat landscape is constantly evolving, with cybercriminals employing increasingly sophisticated methods. Recent trends include targeted ransomware attacks on critical infrastructure, supply chain attacks compromising trusted software, and phishing campaigns exploiting social engineering techniques. These threats not only disrupt operations but also pose significant financial, legal, and reputational risks.

Frameworks for Cybersecurity and Risk Management

Adopting comprehensive frameworks is crucial for effective cybersecurity and risk management. The National Institute of Standards and Technology (NIST) Cybersecurity Framework and the ISO/IEC 27001 standard are widely recognized for establishing robust security practices. These frameworks advocate a holistic approach encompassing identification, protection, detection, response, and recovery from cyber incidents.

Integrating Cybersecurity into Organizational Culture

A strong cybersecurity culture is foundational to effective risk management. This involves fostering awareness and vigilance at all organizational levels, from the boardroom to the front lines. Regular training programs, cybersecurity awareness campaigns, and a clear communication of security policies and procedures are vital in cultivating a culture that prioritizes cybersecurity.

Leveraging Advanced Technologies

Advanced technologies such as Artificial Intelligence (AI), Machine Learning (ML), and blockchain are increasingly being utilized to enhance cybersecurity measures. AI and ML can predict and identify potential threats faster than traditional methods, while blockchain offers a secure and transparent way to manage digital transactions and data storage.

Real-World Scenarios Highlighting the Importance of Cybersecurity and Risk Management

Scenario 1: The SolarWinds Supply Chain Attack

In 2020, a sophisticated supply chain attack on SolarWinds, a company providing network management tools, compromised thousands of organizations worldwide, including government agencies. The attackers inserted malicious code into the software's updates, gaining access to the networks of SolarWinds' customers. This incident underscores the importance of securing the supply chain and adopting a zero-trust security model.

Scenario 2: The Colonial Pipeline Ransomware Attack

In May 2021, a ransomware attack on the Colonial Pipeline, a major fuel pipeline in the United States, led to a temporary shutdown of operations, fuel shortages, and a significant ransom payment. This attack highlights the vulnerability of critical infrastructure to cyber threats and the need for robust incident response plans and cybersecurity measures.

Scenario 3: The Equifax Data Breach

In 2017, Equifax, one of the largest credit reporting agencies, suffered a massive data breach exposing the personal information of approximately 147 million people. The breach was attributed to a failure to patch a known vulnerability. This scenario emphasizes the importance of vulnerability management and regular security assessments to prevent data breaches.

Best Practices for Cybersecurity and Risk Management

1. **Continuous Risk Assessment:** Regularly assess and update the risk profile to reflect changing threat landscapes and business practices.

2. **Incident Response Planning:** Develop and regularly test incident response plans to ensure quick and effective action in the event of a cyber incident.

3. **Data Protection Measures:** Implement strong data encryption, access controls, and data backup strategies to protect sensitive information.

4. **Supplier Risk Management:** Evaluate the cybersecurity practices of suppliers and partners to mitigate supply chain risks.

5. **Regulatory Compliance:** Stay abreast of and comply with relevant cybersecurity regulations and standards to avoid legal penalties and enhance security postures.

Conclusion

Cybersecurity and risk management are not just IT concerns but integral aspects of strategic business planning. The increasing sophistication of cyber threats necessitates a proactive and comprehensive approach to cybersecurity, emphasizing the need for continuous risk assessment, a strong security culture, and the integration of advanced technologies. By drawing lessons from recent cybersecurity incidents and adhering to established best practices, organizations can navigate the digital landscape more securely, protecting their assets and reputation against cyber threats.

Below questions and answers provide a foundation for IT professionals to deepen their understanding and implementation of governance strategies in a digital world, addressing key concerns around alignment, cybersecurity, risk management, and the adoption of emerging technologies.

Questions and Answers

Q1: How can we ensure our IT governance framework remains flexible enough to adapt to rapid technological changes while still aligning with our corporate strategy?

A1: Flexibility can be ensured by adopting agile governance practices that focus on iterative development, feedback loops, and continuous improvement. Incorporate flexible frameworks like COBIT and ITIL, which can be adapted to your organization's changing needs. Regularly review and update your governance framework in response to technological advancements and shifts in corporate strategy. Additionally, fostering a culture of innovation and open communication between IT and business leaders will help identify and adapt to changes more swiftly.

Q2: What are the best practices for integrating cybersecurity and risk management into our corporate strategy?

A2: Best practices include conducting comprehensive risk assessments to identify and prioritize risks and integrating these assessments into the strategic planning process. Adopting recognized cybersecurity frameworks like NIST can guide the development of a robust cybersecurity strategy. Ensure regular communication between cybersecurity teams and strategic planners to align cybersecurity initiatives with business objectives. Also, invest in ongoing employee training and awareness programs to build a culture that values and understands the importance of cybersecurity and risk management.

Q3: How can we effectively measure the success of our IT governance strategy in terms of business value and risk mitigation?

A3: Establish clear, quantifiable key performance indicators (KPIs) that align with both IT and business objectives. These might include metrics related to system uptime, incident response times, customer satisfaction, and financial performance indicators like ROI on IT investments. Regularly review these metrics and adjust strategies as necessary to ensure they continue to support business goals and mitigate risks effectively.

Q4: What steps can we take to cultivate a digital governance culture that embraces change and innovation while managing risks prudently?

A4: Leadership commitment is crucial in shaping a governance culture that balances innovation with risk management. Encourage leaders to champion digital initiatives and demonstrate a commitment to cybersecurity. Implement regular training and awareness programs to enhance employees' understanding of digital risks and governance practices. Promote cross-functional collaboration to break down silos and encourage the sharing of ideas and best practices. Lastly, recognize and reward innovation and prudent risk management to reinforce their value to the organization.

Q5: With the rise of AI, blockchain, and IoT, what are the new governance challenges, and how can we address them?

A5: Emerging technologies introduce challenges related to ethical use, data security, and regulatory compliance. To address these, conduct thorough technology assessments to understand the risks and opportunities each technology presents. Update governance frameworks to include guidelines for the ethical use of AI and blockchain, focusing on transparency, accountability, and data privacy. For IoT, implement robust security protocols and ensure all devices are regularly updated and monitored. Engaging with legal and compliance teams will also ensure that your governance strategies align with current regulations.

Q6: How should we approach global trends and compliance in our digital governance strategies?

A6: Stay informed about global trends and regulatory changes by engaging with industry groups, regulatory bodies, and legal experts. Implement a compliance management system that can adapt to different jurisdictions and regulatory requirements. Regularly review and update your governance and compliance strategies to reflect the latest global trends and regulations. Additionally, consider leveraging technology solutions to automate compliance monitoring and reporting.

Q7: What role do incident response and recovery plans play in our governance strategy, and how can we ensure they are effective?

A7: Incident response and recovery plans are critical for minimizing the impact of security breaches on business operations. Ensure these plans are comprehensive, clearly documented, and regularly tested through drills and simulations. Plans should include clear communication protocols, roles, and responsibilities, as well as procedures for quickly isolating and mitigating breaches. Regularly review and update plans based on lessons learned from tests and actual incidents to ensure they remain effective in rapidly changing threat landscapes.

Case Study: GlobalTech's Digital Governance Transformation

Background

GlobalTech, a leading multinational corporation in the technology sector, recognized the need to overhaul its digital governance framework to align with its aggressive digital transformation strategy. The company aimed to leverage emerging technologies like AI, blockchain, and IoT to drive innovation, improve customer experience, and gain a competitive edge in the market. However, rapid technological changes and the evolving digital threat landscape presented significant challenges.

Challenges

1. **Alignment of IT Governance with Corporate Strategy**: GlobalTech struggled to ensure that its IT governance framework was fully aligned with its corporate strategy, often resulting in misaligned priorities and inefficient allocation of IT resources.

2. **Cybersecurity and Risk Management**: With the adoption of emerging technologies, GlobalTech faced increased cybersecurity threats, including data breaches and compliance risks, which could potentially undermine customer trust and lead to financial losses.

3. **Cultivating a Digital Governance Culture**: Despite recognizing the need for a robust digital governance framework, GlobalTech found it challenging to cultivate a culture that embraced digital transformation while managing risks prudently.

Actions Taken

1. **Strategic Planning and Collaboration**: GlobalTech initiated a series of collaborative workshops between IT and business leaders to define a unified vision and ensure that IT initiatives were directly supporting strategic business objectives.

2. **Adopting and Customizing Governance Frameworks**: The company adopted the COBIT and ITIL frameworks, customizing them to fit its unique needs and ensure a structured approach to managing IT processes aligned with business strategies.

3. **Enhancing Cybersecurity Measures**: GlobalTech adopted the NIST Cybersecurity Framework, focusing on identifying, protecting, detecting, responding to, and recovering from cyber threats. The company also implemented regular cybersecurity training for employees to build awareness.

4. **Agile Governance**: To adapt quickly to market changes and emerging technologies, GlobalTech adopted agile governance practices, focusing on iterative

development, feedback loops, and continuous improvement.

Results

GlobalTech's efforts to align IT governance with its corporate strategy and enhance its cybersecurity and risk management capabilities led to significant improvements in operational efficiency, customer satisfaction, and market competitiveness. The company successfully mitigated several major cybersecurity threats, avoiding potential financial losses and reputational damage. Moreover, the cultivation of a digital governance culture encouraged innovation and prudent risk management across the organization.

Case Study Questions

1. How did GlobalTech's strategic planning and collaboration efforts contribute to aligning IT governance with corporate strategy?

2. What were the key factors in GlobalTech's decision to adopt and customize the COBIT and ITIL frameworks, and how did these frameworks improve its digital governance?

3. Discuss the role of the NIST Cybersecurity Framework in enhancing GlobalTech's cybersecurity measures. What steps did the company take to implement this framework effectively?

4. How did agile governance practices help GlobalTech adapt to rapid market changes and technological advancements? Provide examples of these practices in action.

5. Evaluate the impact of cybersecurity training for employees on GlobalTech's overall security posture.

How can continuous education contribute to a robust digital governance culture?

6. What challenges might GlobalTech face in maintaining its digital governance framework in the future, considering the constant evolution of technology and cyber threats?

7. How can other organizations learn from GlobalTech's approach to digital governance, especially in terms of aligning IT governance with corporate strategy and managing cybersecurity risks?

Chapter 8: Enterprise Architecture in the Age of Digital Transformation

Introduction

The advent of digital transformation has profoundly impacted the way organizations operate, compete, and deliver value to their customers. At the heart of this transformation is the concept of enterprise architecture (EA), which provides a structured framework for integrating and aligning technology, processes, and business strategies. As organizations navigate the complexities of the digital age, the role of enterprise architecture becomes increasingly critical in ensuring agility, innovation, and competitive advantage.

The Evolution of Enterprise Architecture

The Shift Towards Digitalization

The journey towards digital transformation requires a shift from traditional business models to digital-centric strategies. This shift necessitates a reevaluation of existing enterprise architectures to support new business capabilities, such as enhanced customer experiences, data-driven decision-making, and seamless integration of digital technologies.

The Role of EA in Digital Transformation

Enterprise architecture acts as the blueprint for digital transformation, enabling organizations to map out their current state, envision the future state, and plan the transition between the two. By aligning IT infrastructure and services with business goals, EA ensures that digital initiatives are strategically implemented to support overall business objectives.

Strategic Frameworks and Models

TOGAF (The Open Group Architecture Framework)

TOGAF remains one of the most widely adopted frameworks for enterprise architecture. It provides a comprehensive approach to design, planning, implementation, and governance of enterprise IT architecture. In the digital age, TOGAF's iterative process model, the Architecture Development Method (ADM), helps organizations adapt to rapid technological changes while maintaining alignment with business goals.

Zachman Framework

The Zachman Framework offers a structured way of viewing and documenting an organization's enterprise architecture. It is particularly useful in the digital transformation era for its ability to categorize and align different aspects of technology and business processes, ensuring a holistic approach to digital integration.

Aligning Digital Strategies with Business Objectives

Customer-Centric Approaches

Digital transformation is largely driven by the need to enhance customer experiences. Enterprise architecture enables organizations to adopt a customer-centric approach by integrating customer journey mapping and experience design into the strategic planning process. This ensures that technology investments directly contribute to improving customer engagement and satisfaction.

Data-Driven Decision Making

The ability to leverage big data and analytics is a key competitive advantage in the digital era. Enterprise architecture facilitates the integration of data analytics tools and platforms into the organizational infrastructure, enabling data-driven decision making and insights that support strategic business objectives.

Enabling Technologies and Architectures

Cloud Computing

Cloud computing has emerged as a cornerstone of digital transformation, offering scalability, flexibility, and cost-efficiency. Enterprise architecture guides the strategic use of cloud services, ensuring they are aligned with business needs and comply with security and regulatory requirements.

Internet of Things (IoT) and Edge Computing

IoT and edge computing extend the capabilities of enterprise systems to the physical world, enabling real-time data collection and processing. EA frameworks help in designing architectures that seamlessly integrate these technologies, enhancing operational efficiency and creating new business models.

Artificial Intelligence and Machine Learning

AI and ML technologies are pivotal in driving innovation and automation. Through enterprise architecture, organizations can strategically implement AI to optimize processes, enhance customer experiences, and enable predictive analytics, ensuring these technologies align with long-term business strategies.

Governance and Compliance in the Digital Era

Ensuring Security and Privacy

As digital technologies proliferate, so do the risks associated with cybersecurity and data privacy. Enterprise architecture plays a crucial role in establishing governance frameworks that ensure technology implementations are secure, compliant with regulations, and resilient to cyber threats.

Sustainable IT Practices

Sustainability has become a key consideration in digital strategies. Enterprise architecture supports the integration of sustainable IT practices, such as energy-efficient data centers and green computing technologies, aligning digital transformation efforts with environmental and social governance (ESG) goals.

Challenges and Future Directions

Managing Complexity

As digital technologies evolve, organizations face the challenge of managing increasing complexity within their enterprise architecture. Future developments in EA will likely focus on simplifying architectures, enhancing modularity, and promoting interoperability among disparate systems and technologies.

Adapting to Continuous Change

The rapid pace of technological innovation demands that enterprise architectures remain flexible and adaptable. Agile and DevOps methodologies will play a larger role in EA, ensuring that architectures can evolve in response to changing business and technology landscapes.

Designing flexible IT architectures

Designing flexible IT architectures is becoming increasingly crucial as businesses seek to adapt to rapid technological changes, evolving customer expectations, and the need for agility in response to market dynamics. A flexible IT architecture enables organizations to scale, adapt, and integrate new technologies without significant overhauls, ensuring that IT systems can support business growth and transformation effectively.

The essence of a flexible IT architecture lies in its ability to accommodate changes with minimal disruption. This involves adopting modular design principles, leveraging cloud computing, implementing microservices architectures, and ensuring interoperability among systems. By designing IT architectures that are inherently adaptable, organizations can reduce the time and cost associated with implementing new technologies or adjusting to new business requirements.

Moreover, the adoption of open standards and APIs (Application Programming Interfaces) plays a critical role in enhancing flexibility. These technologies allow for seamless integration of disparate systems and applications, facilitating data exchange and workflow automation across different platforms. The use of containerization technologies, such as Docker and Kubernetes, further enhances flexibility by allowing applications to be deployed and managed easily across various environments.

Questions and Answers:

Q1: What role does enterprise architecture (EA) play in the digital transformation of organizations? A1: Enterprise architecture acts as a structured framework for integrating and aligning technology, processes, and business strategies in the digital age. It enables organizations to navigate the complexities of digital transformation by ensuring agility, innovation, and competitive advantage, serving as the blueprint that guides the transition from current to future state while aligning IT infrastructure and services with business goals.

Q2: How has the journey towards digital transformation necessitated a shift in enterprise architecture? A2: The journey towards digital transformation requires moving from traditional business models to digital-centric strategies, demanding a reevaluation of existing enterprise architectures. This shift is essential to support new business capabilities like enhanced customer experiences, data-driven decision-making, and the seamless integration of digital technologies, ensuring that the architecture can accommodate rapid changes and innovations.

Q3: What frameworks support enterprise architecture in the digital transformation era, and how do they assist organizations? A3: Frameworks like TOGAF and the Zachman

Framework support enterprise architecture by providing comprehensive approaches to design, planning, implementation, and governance. TOGAF, with its iterative process model (ADM), helps organizations adapt to technological changes while aligning with business goals. The Zachman Framework offers a structured way to view and document architecture, ensuring a holistic approach to digital integration.

Q4: How does enterprise architecture facilitate a customer-centric approach in digital transformation? A4: Enterprise architecture integrates customer journey mapping and experience design into the strategic planning process, enabling organizations to adopt a customer-centric approach. This ensures that technology investments directly contribute to improving customer engagement and satisfaction, central to digital transformation initiatives.

Q5: In what ways do cloud computing and IoT technologies impact enterprise architecture in the context of digital transformation? A5: Cloud computing offers scalability, flexibility, and cost-efficiency, becoming a cornerstone of digital transformation. IoT and edge computing extend enterprise systems to the physical world, enabling real-time data collection and processing. Enterprise architecture guides the strategic use of these technologies, ensuring alignment with business needs and compliance with security and regulatory requirements.

Q6: Can you provide examples of how organizations successfully transformed their IT architectures and the outcomes they achieved? A6: Netflix's transition to a global streaming service and ING's digital transformation to become more agile and customer-focused are prime examples. Netflix adopted a microservices architecture and leveraged the cloud for scalability and rapid feature deployment, supporting its international expansion. ING restructured its IT around a "banking as a platform" concept, using modular architecture and cloud technologies to innovate and improve customer experiences. These transformations highlight the strategic importance of flexible IT architectures in supporting continuous innovation and operational efficiency.

Q7: What challenges do organizations face in managing the complexity of digital technologies within their enterprise architecture, and how can they adapt? A7: Organizations face the challenge of increasing complexity due to evolving digital technologies. Future developments in enterprise architecture will likely focus on simplifying architectures, enhancing modularity, and promoting interoperability among systems. Adopting Agile and DevOps methodologies can help ensure that architectures remain flexible and adaptable to changing business and technology landscapes.

Following is a case study for the readers based on this chapter and few questions to resolve after the case study.

Case Study: Digital Transformation at TechFusion Inc.

Background: TechFusion Inc. is a global player in the retail industry, facing increased competition from digitally native companies. Recognizing the need to modernize its operations and enhance customer experiences, TechFusion embarked on a digital transformation journey.

Challenge: TechFusion's legacy systems were siloed and inefficient, hindering its ability to adapt to market changes and meet customer expectations. The company needed to overhaul its enterprise architecture to support digital-centric strategies, integrate new technologies seamlessly, and enable data-driven decision-making.

Enterprise Architecture Initiative:

1. **Strategic Framework Adoption**: TechFusion adopted TOGAF as its EA framework to guide the transformation process. The Architecture Development Method (ADM) was utilized to map out the current state, envision the future state, and plan the transition, ensuring IT initiatives were aligned with business goals.

2. **Customer-Centric Approaches**: Incorporating customer journey mapping into the EA strategy, TechFusion redefined its customer engagement models. This shift facilitated the integration of digital technologies like mobile apps and social media, improving customer interaction and satisfaction.

3. **Data-Driven Decision Making**: TechFusion implemented a data analytics platform as part of its EA, enabling insights into customer behavior and market trends. This strategic move fostered informed decision-making, optimized operations, and personalized customer services.

4. **Enabling Technologies**: The company moved its infrastructure to the cloud, leveraging the scalability and flexibility of cloud services. IoT technologies were integrated into the retail stores for real-time inventory tracking, and AI was employed to enhance customer recommendations and operational efficiency.

5. **Governance and Compliance**: A robust governance framework was established to manage the complexities of the new digital ecosystem. This framework ensured security, compliance, and sustainability practices were integrated into the digital transformation efforts.

Outcomes:

- **Enhanced Customer Experience**: TechFusion's digital initiatives led to improved customer satisfaction scores and increased engagement across digital channels.

- **Operational Efficiency**: The integration of IoT and AI technologies streamlined operations, reduced costs, and improved inventory management.

- **Innovation and Agility**: The flexible IT architecture enabled TechFusion to rapidly adapt to market changes and introduce new services, maintaining its competitive edge in the digital era.

Lessons Learned:

- **Continuous Evolution**: TechFusion learned the importance of continuous adaptation, leveraging agile and DevOps methodologies to evolve its enterprise architecture in alignment with emerging technologies and business needs.

- **Collaboration is Key**: Cross-functional collaboration between IT and business units was critical in aligning digital initiatives with strategic objectives, ensuring a unified approach to transformation.

Conclusion: TechFusion Inc.'s journey illustrates the transformative power of enterprise architecture in the digital age. By aligning technology and business strategies through a structured EA framework, organizations can navigate digital transformation complexities, enabling agility, innovation, and sustained competitive advantage.

Case Study Questions

1. What role did TOGAF play in TechFusion Inc.'s digital transformation journey?

2. How did the Architecture Development Method (ADM) facilitate the transition from current to future state architecture?

3. How did integrating customer journey mapping into the enterprise architecture strategy improve customer engagement and satisfaction at TechFusion Inc.?

4. In what ways did implementing a data analytics platform as part of its enterprise architecture enable TechFusion Inc. to achieve data-driven decision-making?

5. How did cloud computing contribute to TechFusion Inc.'s operational efficiency and scalability?

6. What impact did IoT and AI technologies have on TechFusion Inc.'s inventory management and customer service?

7. Describe the governance framework established by TechFusion Inc. to manage digital transformation complexities. How did it ensure security, compliance, and sustainability?

8. What were the key outcomes and benefits of the digital transformation initiative at TechFusion Inc.?

9. How did the enhanced customer experience and operational efficiency contribute to TechFusion Inc.'s competitive advantage in the digital era?

10. What challenges did TechFusion Inc. face during its digital transformation journey, and how were they addressed?

11. Discuss the lessons learned by TechFusion Inc. regarding continuous evolution and the importance of collaboration between IT and business units in digital transformation efforts.

12. Based on the case study, what future directions can be anticipated for enterprise architecture in supporting continuous digital transformation?

13. How can TechFusion Inc. further leverage agile and DevOps methodologies to enhance its enterprise architecture's flexibility and adaptability?

Chapter 9: ITSM and Project Management

Introduction

In the evolving landscape of information technology, the integration of IT Service Management (ITSM) and project management is becoming increasingly crucial for organizations striving to deliver value-driven IT services. This chapter delves into the synergy between ITSM frameworks and project management methodologies, illustrating how their convergence can lead to enhanced efficiency, improved service quality, and alignment with business objectives.

ITSM, at its core, focuses on the management of IT services to meet the needs of the business, emphasizing processes, practices, and policies that support IT operations and service delivery. Project management, on the other hand, is concerned with the planning, executing, and closing of projects to achieve specific goals and meet success criteria within a defined timeline. The intersection of ITSM and project management is where strategic initiatives are efficiently executed, ensuring that IT services are not only reliable and consistent but also align with the changing dynamics of business strategies and goals.

The integration begins with the alignment of ITSM processes with project management activities. For instance, the ITSM process of service strategy can be closely aligned with project initiation and planning phases, ensuring that IT projects are directly contributing to the strategic objectives of the organization. Similarly, the ITSM processes of service design and transition seamlessly integrate with the execution, monitoring, and controlling phases of project management, facilitating a smooth transition of projects from the conceptual stage to operational service.

One of the critical aspects of merging ITSM with project management is the adoption of a shared framework that incorporates best practices from both disciplines. Frameworks such as ITIL (Information Technology Infrastructure Library) for ITSM and PMBOK (Project Management Body of Knowledge) for project management provide comprehensive guidelines and practices that can be tailored to the specific needs of an organization. By leveraging these frameworks, organizations can develop a standardized approach to managing IT projects and services, resulting in improved project outcomes and service quality.

Effective communication and collaboration between ITSM and project management teams are paramount for the successful integration of the two disciplines. Regular meetings, shared tools, and integrated reporting systems can facilitate seamless information flow and coordination, enabling timely decision-making and problem resolution. This collaborative approach not only enhances the efficiency of project execution and service delivery but also fosters a culture of continuous improvement, where lessons learned from projects can be applied to improve ITSM processes and vice versa.

Another significant benefit of integrating ITSM with project management is the enhanced focus on value delivery and customer satisfaction. By aligning IT projects and services with business objectives and customer needs, organizations can ensure that their IT initiatives are delivering tangible value. This customer-centric approach not only improves the quality of IT services but also supports business growth by enabling more agile and responsive IT operations.

Risk management is also a critical area where ITSM and project management intersect. By applying project management principles to ITSM processes, organizations can adopt a proactive approach to identifying, assessing, and mitigating risks associated with IT services and projects. This risk management strategy ensures that potential issues are addressed before they impact service quality or project outcomes, leading to more stable and reliable IT operations.

Agile, Scrum, and Kanban in ITSM

In the chapter on ITSM and Project Management, it's crucial to explore how methodologies like Agile, Scrum, and Kanban are revolutionizing IT Service Management (ITSM). These approaches, rooted in the principles of agility and continuous improvement, offer dynamic frameworks for managing IT projects and services that are in stark contrast to traditional, waterfall methodologies. This section delves into the integration and application of Agile, Scrum, and Kanban within ITSM, highlighting their benefits, challenges, and practical applications.

Agile in ITSM

Agile methodology, with its core principle of adaptability, has significantly influenced ITSM. It promotes a flexible approach to service management, emphasizing the importance of customer collaboration, response to change, and incremental service delivery. Agile in ITSM encourages teams to break down services into manageable parts, allowing for rapid deployment, feedback, and continuous improvement. This adaptability not only enhances service quality but also ensures IT services are more aligned with user needs and business goals.

The Agile Manifesto, with its emphasis on individuals and interactions over processes and tools, working software over comprehensive documentation, customer collaboration over contract negotiation, and responding to change over following a plan, serves as a guiding principle for ITSM teams. By adopting Agile, ITSM can move away from rigid, siloed service management practices to a more collaborative, transparent, and user-focused approach.

Below is the Agile process flow with description

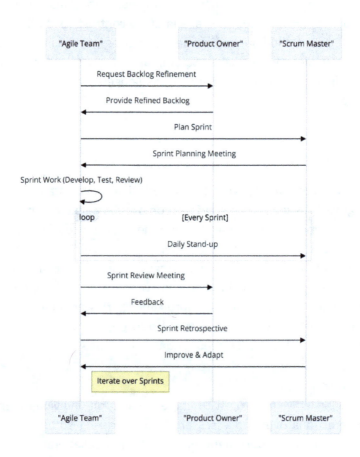

The Agile process depicted in the sequence diagram is centered around iterative development and collaboration. Here's a description of the process flow:

1. **Request Backlog Refinement:** The Agile Team requests the Product Owner (PO) for backlog refinement, signaling the need for clear, prioritized tasks for upcoming sprints.

2. **Provide Refined Backlog:** The Product Owner responds by providing a refined backlog, ensuring that the team has a clear understanding of the project requirements and priorities.

3. **Plan Sprint:** The Agile Team communicates with the Scrum Master (SM) to plan the sprint, which involves defining the sprint goals and selecting tasks from the backlog.

4. **Sprint Planning Meeting:** The Scrum Master facilitates a sprint planning meeting with the team to finalize the sprint backlog and sprint goals.

5. **Sprint Work (Develop, Test, Review):** During the sprint, the team works on the selected tasks, which include development, testing, and reviewing the work to ensure quality and adherence to the sprint goals.

6. **Daily Stand-up:** Throughout the sprint, the team has daily stand-up meetings facilitated by the Scrum Master. These meetings are meant to discuss progress, address any blockers, and adapt the sprint work as needed.

7. **Sprint Review Meeting:** At the end of the sprint, the team presents the completed work to the Product Owner during the sprint review meeting. This is an

opportunity for the PO to provide feedback and for the team to discuss what was accomplished.

8. **Feedback:** Following the sprint review meeting, the Product Owner provides feedback to the team, which is crucial for the iterative improvement of the product.

9. **Sprint Retrospective:** The team then engages in a sprint retrospective meeting led by the Scrum Master. This is a chance to reflect on the sprint process, discuss what went well, what didn't, and identify areas for improvement.

10. **Improve & Adapt:** Finally, based on the insights gained from the retrospective, the team aims to implement changes to improve and adapt their process for the next sprint.

This cycle repeats for each sprint, allowing the team to continuously improve their process and product incrementally.

Scrum in ITSM

Scrum, a subset of Agile, introduces a structured yet flexible framework for managing complex projects. In ITSM, Scrum can facilitate the rapid development and delivery of IT services. Scrum roles (Product Owner, Scrum Master, and Development Team), artifacts (Product Backlog, Sprint Backlog, and Increment), and ceremonies (Sprint Planning, Daily Stand-up, Sprint Review, and Sprint Retrospective) can be adapted to fit the ITSM context.

Incorporating Scrum into ITSM, service management teams can work in sprints, typically lasting two to four weeks, allowing for frequent reassessment and realignment of IT services with business objectives. This iterative process enables the continuous delivery of value to customers, with each sprint aiming to produce a potentially shippable increment of a service. The Scrum framework fosters a culture of transparency, inspection, and adaptation, which is vital for the dynamic nature of IT services.

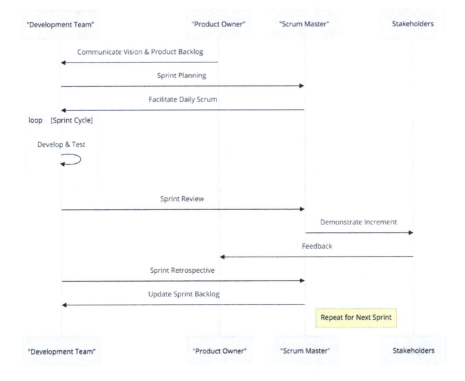

The Scrum process described in the diagram involves the following steps:

1. **Communicate Vision & Product Backlog:** The Product Owner communicates the project vision and product backlog to the Development Team. This includes all the tasks and features that need to be developed.

2. **Sprint Planning:** The Development Team, with the guidance of the Scrum Master, conducts sprint planning to select items from the product backlog to work on during the sprint.

3. **Facilitate Daily Scrum:** The Scrum Master facilitates daily scrum meetings where the Development Team discusses progress and any impediments to their tasks.

4. **Develop & Test:** Within the sprint cycle, the Development Team works on the tasks, developing and testing the features.

5. **Sprint Review:** At the end of the sprint, the Development Team presents the increment to the Scrum Master during the sprint review.

6. **Demonstrate Increment:** The Scrum Master then demonstrates the work completed during the sprint to the stakeholders, collecting their feedback.

7. **Feedback:** The feedback from stakeholders is communicated back to the Product Owner.

8. **Sprint Retrospective:** The Development Team and the Scrum Master conduct a sprint retrospective to reflect on the sprint, discussing what went well and what could be improved.

9. **Update Sprint Backlog:** Based on the retrospective and feedback, the Scrum Master helps the team update the sprint backlog for the next sprint.

10. **Repeat for Next Sprint:** The cycle repeats with the next sprint planning, ensuring continuous improvement and adaptation based on feedback and reflection.

This iterative cycle enables the Scrum Team to adapt to changes quickly and efficiently, maintaining a focus on delivering the highest value to the stakeholders.

Kanban in ITSM

Kanban, another Agile methodology, offers a visual approach to managing work as it moves through a process. Kanban visualizes both the process (the workflow) and the actual work passing through that process. The goal of Kanban is to identify potential bottlenecks in the process and fix them so work can flow through it cost-effectively at an optimal speed or throughput. In ITSM, Kanban can be particularly effective in managing ongoing and operational tasks such as incident management, problem management, and request fulfillment.

The Kanban board, with its columns representing different stages of the workflow, allows ITSM teams to visualize service requests and monitor their progress from initiation to completion. This visual management supports just-in-time delivery and helps in managing workloads, reducing cycle times, and improving service delivery efficiency. By limiting work in progress (WIP), Kanban encourages teams to focus on completing current tasks before taking on new ones, thereby increasing efficiency and reducing the time to deliver IT services.

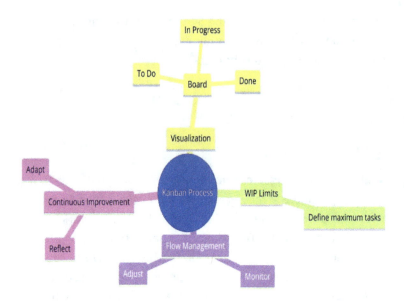

Kanban Process Description:

The Kanban process is a method for managing work by balancing demands with available capacity and improving the handling of system-level bottlenecks. Here's a breakdown based on the mindmap:

1. **Visualization:** The core of the Kanban process is visualizing the work as it moves through the process. This is usually done with a Kanban board that has columns such as "To Do," "In Progress," and "Done."

2. **WIP Limits (Work In Progress Limits):** WIP limits are critical in Kanban to ensure that teams do not overcommit. They define the maximum number of tasks in different stages of the workflow to prevent bottlenecks.

3. **Flow Management:** This involves monitoring the flow of work items through the process and adjusting as necessary to improve efficiency. It focuses on ensuring that tasks move smoothly from start to finish without unnecessary delays.

4. **Continuous Improvement:** Kanban is an evolutionary method that encourages continuous small changes to the current process. Teams regularly reflect on their workflow, the effectiveness of their work, and adapt their practices to improve efficiency and productivity.

Integrating Agile, Scrum, and Kanban with ITSM

Integrating Agile, Scrum, and Kanban methodologies into ITSM processes requires a cultural shift within the organization. It involves moving away from traditional, hierarchical structures to more collaborative, cross-functional teams. Training and coaching are essential to help teams understand and adopt these methodologies. Moreover, ITSM tools and technologies should support Agile practices, facilitating collaboration, automation, and real-time reporting.

The integration of Agile, Scrum, and Kanban into ITSM brings several benefits, including increased flexibility, improved customer satisfaction, faster delivery of services, and a more responsive IT service management framework. However, organizations must be mindful of the challenges, such as resistance to change, the need for continuous improvement, and the importance of maintaining alignment with business objectives.

In conclusion, Agile, Scrum, and Kanban methodologies offer valuable frameworks for enhancing ITSM practices. By adopting these approaches, ITSM can become more dynamic, user-centered, and aligned with the fast-paced nature of today's business environment. This integration not only improves the delivery and management of IT services but also fosters a culture of continuous improvement and innovation within IT service management.

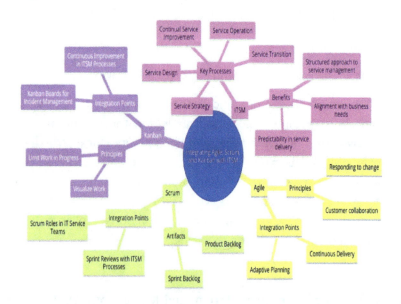

Description of the Integration Process:

Agile Integration:

- **Principles:** Emphasizes customer collaboration and responding to change.

- **Integration Points:** Integrates with ITSM through continuous delivery and adaptive planning, enhancing flexibility and responsiveness in service management.

Scrum Integration:

- **Artifacts:** Includes the product backlog and sprint backlog as key components.

- **Integration Points:** Scrum can be integrated into ITSM by aligning sprint reviews with ITSM processes and adapting Scrum roles for IT service teams, improving project management within IT services.

Kanban Integration:

- **Principles:** Focuses on visualizing work and limiting work in progress.

- **Integration Points:** Kanban boards can be used for incident management and continuous improvement processes within ITSM, aiding in task management and process optimization.

ITSM Core Processes:

- **Key Processes:** Encompasses service strategy, service design, service transition, service operation, and continual service improvement.

- **Benefits:** Offers a structured approach to service management, ensuring alignment with business needs and predictability in service delivery.

This integration aims to combine the strengths of Agile, Scrum, and Kanban methodologies with ITSM's structured approach to service management, resulting in improved efficiency, flexibility, and responsiveness in delivering IT services.

Balancing Traditional and Agile Methodologies in ITSM

In the evolving field of IT Service Management (ITSM), the challenge of balancing traditional and agile methodologies represents a critical junction in the chapter on ITSM and Project Management. Traditional methodologies, often characterized by their structured and linear approach, such as the Waterfall model, have provided a foundation for ITSM practices for decades. Conversely, agile methodologies, with their flexible, iterative approach, have introduced a dynamic capability to adapt to changing requirements and foster continuous improvement. This section explores the strategies and considerations necessary to blend these methodologies effectively, ensuring a comprehensive, resilient, and adaptable ITSM framework.

The Need for Balance

The drive to integrate traditional and agile methodologies stems from the need to combine the stability and predictability of traditional approaches with the flexibility and responsiveness of agile practices. Traditional methodologies excel in environments where requirements are well-defined and changes are minimal, offering a clear, sequential progression of project phases. However, in the fast-paced and often unpredictable realm of IT services, the ability to adapt quickly to new information, changing requirements, and emerging technologies is paramount. Agile methodologies cater to this need, emphasizing rapid iteration, stakeholder collaboration, and a focus on delivering value early and continuously.

Balancing these methodologies allows ITSM to leverage the strengths of each, applying them where they fit best within the service lifecycle. This blended approach can lead to more efficient service design, development, and delivery, enhancing customer satisfaction and aligning IT services more closely with business goals.

Strategies for Integration

The integration of traditional and agile methodologies within ITSM requires a thoughtful approach, tailored to the organization's specific context, culture, and objectives. Several strategies can facilitate this balance:

- **Hybrid Models:** Develop a hybrid ITSM model that incorporates elements of both traditional and agile methodologies. For example, use a traditional approach for the initial planning and design phases, ensuring compliance and alignment with strategic objectives, then switch to agile methodologies for development and implementation, allowing for flexibility and rapid iteration.

- **Phased Implementation:** Gradually introduce agile practices into traditional ITSM processes. Start with projects or areas where the benefits of agility are most apparent, such as software development or new service innovation, before expanding to other areas.

- **Flexible Frameworks:** Adopt flexible ITSM frameworks that can accommodate both traditional and agile practices. ITIL 4, for instance, introduces concepts that support agility within ITSM, such as the Service Value Chain, which can adapt to different approaches for creating, delivering, and supporting IT services.

- **Cultural Shift:** Foster a culture that values both stability and adaptability. Encourage open communication, collaboration, and continuous learning among ITSM teams. The success of blending methodologies depends significantly on the willingness of individuals and teams to embrace both structured and flexible ways of working.

- **Tooling and Technology:** Implement ITSM tools and technologies that support both methodologies. Look for features that facilitate project management, collaboration, real-time reporting, and automation, allowing teams to apply the most appropriate approach for each task or project phase.

Challenges and Considerations

While the integration of traditional and agile methodologies presents numerous benefits, it also poses challenges. Resistance to change, especially from teams accustomed to one methodology over the other, can hinder integration efforts. Additionally, balancing the rigor and documentation requirements of traditional approaches with the fast-paced, iterative nature of agile practices requires careful management to avoid conflicts and inefficiencies.

To address these challenges, organizations should prioritize clear communication, outlining the benefits and rationale for integrating methodologies. Training and education can equip teams with the skills and mindset needed to navigate both traditional and agile approaches effectively. Furthermore, leadership support is crucial in driving the cultural and procedural changes necessary for successful integration.

Conclusion

Balancing traditional and agile methodologies within ITSM offers a pathway to more resilient, responsive, and effective IT service management. By strategically integrating these approaches, organizations can harness the strengths of each, delivering IT services that are both reliable and adaptable to the ever-changing demands of the business environment. This balance not only enhances the efficiency and quality of IT services but also positions ITSM as a key enabler of business innovation and growth.

Questions and Answers for "ITSM and Project Management"

1. How do ITSM and project management complement each other in delivering IT services?

Answer: ITSM and project management complement each other by combining the structured approach of ITSM for managing services with the strategic execution capabilities of project management. While ITSM focuses on ensuring IT services meet business needs through standardized processes and practices, project management concentrates on planning, executing, and finalizing projects within specific timelines and objectives. Their integration ensures IT services are not only reliable and consistent but also align with dynamic business strategies and goals, enhancing efficiency and service quality.

2. What are some benefits of integrating Agile methodologies with ITSM?

Answer: Integrating Agile methodologies with ITSM brings several benefits, including increased flexibility, faster delivery of services, improved customer satisfaction, and a more responsive IT service management framework. Agile's adaptability allows teams to respond quickly to changes and customer needs, while its emphasis on collaboration and continuous improvement helps refine ITSM processes. This integration fosters a dynamic, customer-focused approach to managing and delivering IT services.

3. Can you explain how Scrum can be adapted to fit within an ITSM context?

Answer: Scrum can be adapted to fit within an ITSM context by applying Its structured yet flexible framework to the service management lifecycle. In ITSM, Scrum roles such as Product Owner, Scrum Master, and Development Team can oversee service development and delivery. The use of Scrum artifacts and ceremonies, like Sprints, Sprint Planning, and Retrospectives, can facilitate rapid development, frequent reassessment, and continuous improvement of IT services. This adaptation allows ITSM teams to work in sprints, aligning IT services more closely with business objectives and customer needs.

4. How does Kanban improve service delivery efficiency in ITSM?

Answer: Kanban improves service delivery efficiency in ITSM by providing a visual method to manage and optimize workflow processes. By visualizing the flow of work on a Kanban board, ITSM teams can easily identify bottlenecks, manage workloads, and prioritize tasks. This method supports just-in-time delivery, reduces cycle times, and increases efficiency, allowing teams to focus on completing current tasks before taking on new ones. Kanban's emphasis on limiting work in progress ensures a more efficient and timely delivery of IT services.

5. What are some challenges organizations might face when integrating ITSM with project management, and how can they be addressed?

Answer: Challenges in integrating ITSM with project management include resistance to change, skill gaps among team members, and the complexity of aligning different methodologies. These can be addressed by:

- Providing comprehensive training and resources to develop necessary skills.

- Clearly communicating the benefits and rationale for integration to all stakeholders.

- Gradually introducing changes to allow teams to adapt to new processes.

- Leveraging leadership support to drive cultural and procedural changes.

- Implementing flexible frameworks and tools that support both ITSM and project management practices.

6. How can Agile, Scrum, and Kanban methodologies be integrated into ITSM processes?

Answer: Agile, Scrum, and Kanban methodologies can be integrated into ITSM processes by:

- Adopting Agile principles such as adaptability, customer collaboration, and response to change to enhance service management practices.

- Applying Scrum's structured framework to manage complex IT service projects, utilizing roles, artifacts, and ceremonies to facilitate rapid development and delivery.

- Using Kanban to visually manage and optimize ITSM workflows, identifying and addressing bottlenecks for more efficient service delivery. This integration requires a cultural shift within the organization, training for team members, and the adoption of tools that support Agile practices.

7. What role does effective communication play in the successful integration of ITSM and project management?

Answer: Effective communication is paramount for the successful integration of ITSM and project management. It ensures that all stakeholders, including development and operations teams, are aligned with the project's objectives and understand their roles and responsibilities. Regular meetings, shared tools, and integrated reporting systems facilitate seamless information flow and coordination, enabling timely decision-making and problem resolution. This collaborative approach enhances project execution efficiency and fosters a culture of continuous improvement.

8. Discuss the importance of balancing traditional and agile methodologies in ITSM.

Answer: Balancing traditional and agile methodologies in ITSM is crucial for creating a comprehensive, resilient, and adaptable service management framework. Traditional methodologies offer stability and predictability, ideal for well-defined requirements and minimal changes. In contrast, agile methodologies provide the flexibility and responsiveness needed to adapt to rapid changes and emerging technologies. By balancing these approaches, ITSM can leverage the strengths of each to design, develop, and deliver services more efficiently, meeting both customer satisfaction and business objectives.

Case Study: GlobalTech's Journey to Integrating ITSM and Agile Project Management

Background

GlobalTech, a multinational corporation specializing in IT solutions and services, faced significant challenges in responding to the rapidly changing demands of the technology sector. Their traditional IT Service Management (ITSM) framework, while robust, was proving to be too rigid and slow, leading to delays in service delivery and dissatisfaction among clients. To address these issues, GlobalTech decided to embark on a journey to integrate Agile project management methodologies into their existing ITSM processes.

Challenge

The primary challenge GlobalTech faced was the resistance to change within its organization. The IT department was deeply rooted in traditional methodologies, with well-established

128

processes and a culture that valued predictability and control over flexibility and rapid response. Furthermore, there was a lack of understanding and experience with Agile methodologies among staff, raising concerns about the potential disruption to ongoing operations and service delivery.

Solution

GlobalTech's approach to integrating Agile methodologies into its ITSM framework involved several key strategies:

1. **Executive Sponsorship and Training:** Recognizing the importance of leadership support, GlobalTech's executive team sponsored the initiative, ensuring it received the necessary resources and visibility. They also invested in comprehensive training programs to build Agile capabilities across the organization.

2. **Pilot Projects:** GlobalTech selected a few pilot projects to introduce Agile practices, choosing initiatives that would benefit most from flexibility and rapid iteration. This approach allowed the organization to test and refine the integration of Agile and ITSM in a controlled environment.

3. **Hybrid Framework Development:** Working with Agile coaches and ITSM experts, GlobalTech developed a hybrid framework that combined the strengths of both methodologies. This framework emphasized collaboration, customer feedback, and continuous improvement, while maintaining the control and structure necessary for IT service management.

4. **Cultural Transformation:** Understanding that the success of the initiative depended on a shift in organizational culture, GlobalTech launched a series of workshops and communication campaigns to promote

the values of agility, such as openness to change, collaboration, and customer focus.

5. **Continuous Improvement:** GlobalTech established a feedback loop, using insights from pilot projects to refine their approach. Regular retrospectives and lessons learned sessions became a part of the culture, fostering an environment of continuous improvement.

Results

Within a year of implementing the hybrid ITSM-Agile framework, GlobalTech saw significant improvements in its service delivery and project management capabilities. Service delivery times were reduced by 30%, and customer satisfaction scores increased significantly. The organization became more adaptable, able to respond to changes in customer requirements and market conditions more swiftly. Moreover, the initiative fostered a more collaborative and innovative culture within the IT department, with teams more engaged and motivated than ever before.

Reflection

GlobalTech's journey underscores the importance of flexibility, leadership, and a commitment to continuous improvement in integrating Agile methodologies with traditional ITSM frameworks. The case study demonstrates that while challenges are inevitable, the benefits of a more responsive and customer-focused approach to IT service management are substantial.

Below are the questions for you to answer after reading the case study.

1. How did GlobalTech address the challenge of cultural resistance to Agile methodologies within its organization?
2. What were the key factors in selecting pilot projects for the integration of Agile and ITSM at GlobalTech?

3. Describe the hybrid framework developed by GlobalTech. What elements of Agile and ITSM were combined, and how did this benefit the organization?
4. Discuss the role of continuous improvement in GlobalTech's integration of Agile methodologies into its ITSM processes. How did the organization ensure that improvements were ongoing?
5. Reflecting on GlobalTech's experience, what lessons can be learned about integrating Agile methodologies into traditional ITSM frameworks?
6. How did GlobalTech measure the success of integrating Agile into its ITSM processes, and what impact did this have on service delivery and customer satisfaction?
7. In what ways did executive sponsorship contribute to the success of GlobalTech's Agile-ITSM integration initiative?
8. Considering GlobalTech's journey, what recommendations would you make to other organizations looking to integrate Agile methodologies into their ITSM frameworks?

Chapter 10: DevOps: A Synergistic Approach

Introduction

In an era defined by rapid technological advancement and shifting market dynamics, the role of the Chief Information Officer (CIO) is increasingly complex and critical. As organizations strive to remain competitive and innovative, the integration of Information Technology Service Management (ITSM) with modern methodologies like DevOps has become paramount. This chapter delves into the DevOps approach, emphasizing its significance for CIOs tasked with navigating the challenges and opportunities presented by AI, automation, and beyond. We explore the genesis of DevOps, its core principles, and its transformative potential for ITSM, providing insights into how CIOs can harness this synergy to drive their organizations forward.

Understanding DevOps

At its heart, DevOps is a cultural and professional movement that promotes collaboration between development and operations teams to automate the process of software delivery and infrastructure changes. It aims to build, test, and release software more rapidly, frequently, and reliably by embracing a set of practices that bring together technology operations and software development.

The Genesis and Evolution of DevOps

The DevOps movement emerged from the need to overcome the limitations of traditional software development and delivery models, which often led to silos between developers and operations teams. This siloed approach resulted in bottlenecks, misunderstandings, and delays. DevOps arose as a solution, fostering a culture of collaboration, shared responsibility, and continuous improvement.

Core Principles of DevOps

The DevOps methodology is underpinned by several key principles, often summarized by the acronym CAMS: Culture, Automation, Measurement, and Sharing.

- **Culture:** DevOps advocates for a shift in mindset, emphasizing collaboration, openness, and mutual respect among all stakeholders involved in the development, delivery, and management of IT services.
- **Automation:** To achieve speed and efficiency, DevOps relies heavily on automating repetitive tasks in the software development lifecycle, from integration, testing, and deployment to infrastructure provisioning and management.
- **Measurement:** Continuous improvement in DevOps is driven by a rigorous focus on measurement and metrics. Performance indicators such as deployment frequency, change failure rates, and time to recovery are critical for assessing progress and identifying areas for enhancement.
- **Sharing:** Knowledge sharing and transparency are fundamental to the DevOps ethos, breaking down traditional barriers and fostering a culture where learning from failures and successes is encouraged.

DevOps and ITSM: Synergizing for the Future

The integration of DevOps with ITSM frameworks like ITIL offers a powerful combination for CIOs. ITSM provides a structured approach to managing IT services, focusing on aligning IT processes and services with business objectives. DevOps injects agility, speed, and innovation into this framework, addressing the demand for faster service delivery and continuous improvement. This synergy enables organizations to not only maintain robust service management practices but also to adapt quickly to changing needs and technologies.

Navigating the Age of AI and Automation

The advent of AI and automation technologies has further underscored the value of a DevOps approach. AI can enhance DevOps practices by providing insights into system performance, predicting potential issues, and automating decision-making processes. In turn, DevOps ensures that AI and automation are integrated smoothly into IT operations, enhancing efficiency and enabling more sophisticated, data-driven decision-making.

Implementing a DevOps Culture: Challenges and Opportunities

For CIOs, leading the transition to a DevOps culture involves navigating several challenges, including overcoming resistance to change, upskilling teams, and selecting the right tools and technologies. Success requires a clear vision, strong leadership, and a commitment to fostering an environment where continuous learning and collaboration are valued.

Measuring Success and Continuous Improvement

Implementing DevOps is a journey, not a destination. CIOs must establish clear metrics to measure the impact of DevOps practices on service delivery, operational efficiency, and customer satisfaction. Regularly reviewing these metrics, soliciting feedback, and being open to adjustments are crucial for continuous improvement and alignment with business goals.

As we delve deeper into the transformative power of DevOps within the realm of IT Service Management (ITSM), it's essential to underscore the practical implications, examples, and detailed strategies that can guide CIOs in leveraging this approach. This expanded discussion will explore real-world applications of DevOps, the integration of cutting-edge technologies, and the steps for fostering a culture that embraces change and innovation.

Real-World Applications of DevOps

Example 1: Financial Services Firm Embraces DevOps for Faster Service Delivery

A leading financial services firm faced challenges in meeting the rapidly changing demands of its customers due to slow software development cycles and cumbersome release processes. By adopting a DevOps approach, the firm implemented continuous integration and continuous delivery (CI/CD) pipelines, automating the build, test, and deployment processes. This shift not only accelerated software deployment from months to weeks but also significantly reduced deployment failures and downtime. Collaboration between development and operations teams improved, leading to a more agile response to market changes and customer needs.

Example 2: Retail Giant Utilizes DevOps for Scalability and Efficiency

A global retail company struggling with scalability issues, especially during peak shopping seasons, turned to DevOps to enhance its IT infrastructure's responsiveness and efficiency. The company employed infrastructure as code (IaC) to automate the provisioning and management of cloud resources, ensuring scalability and flexibility. Through DevOps practices, the retailer achieved a significant reduction in infrastructure provisioning time from days to minutes, enabling it to dynamically adjust to fluctuating demand and improve customer experience.

Leveraging AI and Automation in DevOps

AI-Driven Predictive Analytics for Proactive Issue Resolution

By integrating AI-driven predictive analytics into their DevOps strategy, organizations can anticipate and mitigate potential issues before they impact operations. For instance, AI algorithms can analyze patterns from historical incident data to predict system failures, allowing teams to proactively address vulnerabilities and reduce downtime.

Automation for Enhanced Efficiency

Automation in DevOps extends beyond CI/CD pipelines. For example, chatbots and virtual assistants can automate routine inquiries and tasks, freeing up human resources for more complex problems. Additionally, automated security testing tools can be integrated into the development lifecycle, ensuring that security is a shared responsibility and is addressed continuously.

Steps for Fostering a DevOps Culture

1. **Leadership Commitment**: The transition to a DevOps culture starts with commitment from the top. CIOs must champion the cause, demonstrating the value of DevOps in achieving business goals and fostering an environment that encourages experimentation and learning from failures.
2. **Education and Training**: Investing in education and training is critical to equip teams with the necessary skills and knowledge. This includes not only technical training on tools and practices but also workshops on collaboration, communication, and agile methodologies.
3. **Cross-Functional Teams**: Encourage the formation of cross-functional teams that include members from development, operations, quality assurance, security, and business units. These teams should work towards shared objectives, breaking down traditional silos.
4. **Implement Toolchains**: Select and implement a set of tools that support the DevOps methodology, including

version control, continuous integration, deployment automation, and monitoring. These tools should be integrated to create a seamless pipeline that facilitates collaboration and automation.

5. **Continuous Feedback and Improvement**: Establish mechanisms for continuous feedback from end-users and stakeholders. Use this feedback, along with performance metrics, to drive continuous improvement in processes, products, and services.

Principles of DevOps in ITSM

The integration of DevOps principles into IT Service Management (ITSM) represents a fundamental shift towards a more agile, responsive, and efficient approach to delivering IT services. At its core, DevOps aims to break down the silos between development and operations, fostering a culture of collaboration, continuous improvement, and high performance. The principles of DevOps, when thoughtfully applied to ITSM, can dramatically transform service delivery, enhance customer satisfaction, and drive business value.

Culture of Collaboration and Communication
A pivotal principle of DevOps is fostering a culture where open communication and collaboration are the norms. In ITSM, this means creating environments where development, operations, and support teams work closely together throughout the service lifecycle. By promoting a unified culture, organizations can ensure that IT services are developed, deployed, and managed with a shared understanding of business objectives and customer needs.

Automation and Continuous Delivery
DevOps emphasizes the importance of automating the software delivery pipeline to achieve continuous integration (CI) and continuous delivery (CD). In the context of ITSM, automation extends beyond software deployment to include processes like incident management, change management, and configuration management. Automating these processes reduces manual

errors, speeds up service delivery, and enables IT teams to focus on higher-value activities.

Lean Management

Adopting lean principles from DevOps means streamlining ITSM processes to eliminate waste, improve efficiency, and deliver value more quickly. This involves continuously reviewing and refining ITSM processes to ensure they are as efficient as possible, removing unnecessary steps, and optimizing resource utilization.

Measurement and Feedback

Continuous measurement and feedback are central to DevOps and critical for ITSM integration. This principle involves establishing key performance indicators (KPIs) and metrics to track the effectiveness of IT services and processes. Regularly collecting and analyzing data provides insights into areas for improvement, helping teams to make informed decisions and adapt their strategies to enhance service quality and performance.

Sharing and Knowledge Management

Knowledge sharing is a fundamental aspect of DevOps that enriches ITSM practices. It involves creating platforms and practices for sharing best practices, lessons learned, and innovations across teams. This open exchange of knowledge not only accelerates problem-solving and innovation but also contributes to building a resilient and adaptable IT organization.

Real-world Implementation Strategies

Implementing DevOps principles within ITSM requires a strategic and thoughtful approach. The following strategies provide a roadmap for organizations looking to embark on this transformative journey.

Assess and Plan

Begin with a thorough assessment of current ITSM processes, tools, and culture. Identify areas where DevOps principles can have the most significant impact and align with business objectives. Develop a strategic plan that outlines the goals, milestones, and key performance indicators (KPIs) for the integration.

Build Cross-Functional Teams
Create cross-functional teams that include members from development, operations, and other relevant areas. These teams should be empowered to manage IT services from development through to operations, fostering a sense of ownership and collaboration. Encourage regular communication and knowledge sharing within and between teams to break down silos.

Automate ITSM Processes
Identify ITSM processes that can be automated to improve efficiency and accuracy. Implement tools and technologies that support automation, such as CI/CD tools for software deployment, automated testing tools, and configuration management tools. Ensure that automation efforts are aligned with the overall ITSM strategy and business objectives.

Foster a Culture of Continuous Improvement
Cultivate an organizational culture that embraces continuous improvement. Encourage experimentation, tolerate failures as learning opportunities, and celebrate successes. Implement regular retrospectives and feedback loops to identify areas for improvement and make incremental changes to processes and practices.

Train and Upskill Teams
Invest in training and development programs to upskill teams in DevOps practices and tools. Provide opportunities for learning and growth, including workshops, certifications, and cross-training initiatives. Ensure that teams have the skills and

knowledge needed to implement and sustain DevOps principles within ITSM.

Measure and Adjust
Regularly measure the impact of DevOps integration on ITSM processes and service delivery. Use the established KPIs and metrics to assess performance, identify areas for improvement, and demonstrate value to stakeholders. Be prepared to adjust strategies and practices based on feedback and performance data to continuously enhance service delivery.

Share Knowledge and Successes
Promote a culture of knowledge sharing by documenting best practices, lessons learned, and success stories. Use internal platforms, meetings, and workshops to share insights and experiences across the organization. This not only accelerates learning and improvement but also helps to sustain the momentum of the DevOps integration effort.

Integrating DevOps principles into ITSM is a journey that requires commitment, patience, and continuous learning. By adopting these strategies, organizations can navigate the complexities of this integration, unlocking the potential to deliver superior IT services that are agile, efficient, and closely aligned with business needs and customer expectations.

Questions and Answers:

1. What is DevOps and why is it important in the current IT landscape?

Answer: DevOps is a set of practices that combines software development (Dev) and IT operations (Ops) aimed at shortening the system development life cycle and providing continuous delivery with high software quality. It is important in the current

IT landscape because it enhances collaboration between teams, improves efficiencies, accelerates time to market, and responds more effectively to customer needs.

2. How does DevOps complement ITSM?

Answer: DevOps complements ITSM by introducing agility and flexibility into the structured and process-oriented approach of ITSM. While ITSM focuses on aligning IT services with business needs, DevOps brings in practices for faster development and deployment, ensuring that IT services are delivered more efficiently and are continuously improved upon. The synergy between DevOps and ITSM supports a more dynamic IT service management framework that can adapt to rapid changes and innovate in response to evolving business requirements.

3. Can you explain the core principles of DevOps?

Answer: The core principles of DevOps, often encapsulated by the acronym CAMS, include Culture, Automation, Measurement, and Sharing:

- **Culture:** Promotes collaboration and communication between development, operations, and other stakeholders in the organization.

- **Automation:** Focuses on automating the software delivery process to improve efficiency and consistency.

- **Measurement:** Involves tracking and analyzing data to make informed decisions and improvements.

- **Sharing:** Encourages sharing knowledge and best practices to enhance team synergy and innovation.

4. What role does automation play in DevOps?

Answer: Automation is a cornerstone of DevOps, facilitating continuous integration, continuous delivery, and rapid feedback mechanisms. It streamlines processes such as code integration, testing, deployment, and infrastructure provisioning, which significantly reduces manual errors, increases efficiency, and allows teams to focus on higher-value tasks. Automation ensures that software can be developed, tested, and released faster and more reliably.

5. How does DevOps impact organizational culture?

Answer: DevOps significantly impacts organizational culture by fostering a collaborative environment that breaks down silos between development and operations teams. It encourages open communication, shared responsibility for the product's success, and a culture of continuous improvement. This cultural shift promotes innovation, accelerates problem-solving, and enhances job satisfaction among team members.

6. What are some challenges of implementing DevOps in an organization?

Answer: Some challenges include cultural resistance, as shifting to a DevOps model requires changes in traditional workflows and mindsets. Skill gaps may also pose a challenge, requiring training and possibly hiring new talent familiar with DevOps practices. Additionally, selecting and integrating the right set of tools to support DevOps processes can be complex and time-consuming.

7. How do you measure the success of a DevOps implementation?

Answer: Success can be measured through various key performance indicators (KPIs), such as deployment frequency, time to market, change failure rate, mean time to recovery (MTTR), and overall improvement in software quality and stability. Customer satisfaction and feedback can also be valuable metrics to assess the impact of DevOps practices on product delivery and service improvement.

8. What strategies can organizations use to foster a DevOps culture?

Answer: Organizations can foster a DevOps culture by:

- Providing training and resources to develop the necessary skills.

- Encouraging collaboration and communication across departments.

- Implementing tools that facilitate automation and continuous delivery.

- Establishing metrics and feedback loops for continuous improvement.

- Celebrating successes and learning from failures to encourage innovation and risk-taking.

9. Can DevOps and ITSM coexist in an organization?

Answer: Yes, DevOps and ITSM can coexist and complement each other in an organization. ITSM provides a structured approach to managing IT services and aligning them with business needs, while DevOps introduces practices that improve the speed, efficiency, and quality of software delivery. Together, they create a comprehensive framework for delivering IT services that are both agile and aligned with business objectives.

10. How does automation in DevOps differ from traditional IT automation?

Answer: Automation in DevOps focuses on the entire software delivery pipeline, including development, testing, deployment, and operations, to enable continuous integration and continuous delivery. It is more comprehensive and integrated than traditional IT automation, which often focuses on automating specific, standalone tasks. DevOps automation aims to create a seamless, automated workflow that enhances speed, reliability, and scalability in software delivery and infrastructure management.

Case Study: Transforming AcmeCorp with DevOps

Background

AcmeCorp, a global financial services provider, faced growing challenges in its IT operations, struggling with long development cycles, frequent service disruptions, and a growing backlog of customer feature requests. With the industry rapidly evolving, AcmeCorp recognized the need to innovate its IT service delivery to stay competitive. The company decided to embark on a transformative journey by integrating DevOps practices into its existing ITSM framework.

Challenge

AcmeCorp's traditional ITSM approach, while robust, was siloed and lacked the agility needed to respond to fast-changing market demands. Development and operations teams worked separately, leading to delays, miscommunication, and a slow response to issues and updates. The company needed a strategy to accelerate its service delivery without sacrificing quality or stability.

Solution

AcmeCorp launched a comprehensive DevOps initiative, focusing on the following key strategies:

1. **Cultural Transformation:** AcmeCorp began with workshops and training sessions to foster a culture of collaboration, continuous improvement, and shared responsibility across development and operations teams.

2. **Automation of the Delivery Pipeline:** The company implemented tools for continuous integration and continuous delivery (CI/CD), automating code integration, testing, and deployment processes. This reduced manual errors and significantly accelerated the delivery timeline.

3. **Enhanced Monitoring and Feedback Loops:** By adopting real-time monitoring tools and establishing feedback loops, AcmeCorp enabled its teams to quickly identify and address issues, leading to improved service reliability and customer satisfaction.

4. **Iterative Improvements:** Adopting an iterative approach, AcmeCorp focused on making small, incremental changes, allowing for quick wins and continuous refinement of processes and services.

Results

Within a year of implementing DevOps practices, AcmeCorp witnessed transformative results:

- **Deployment Frequency:** The frequency of deployments increased from monthly to daily, enabling quicker delivery of features and fixes to customers.

- **Service Stability:** Incident recovery times improved by 70%, and the change failure rate decreased significantly.

- **Customer Satisfaction:** Feedback loops and faster service improvements led to a 40% increase in customer satisfaction scores.

- **Collaboration and Morale:** Enhanced collaboration and a culture of continuous improvement boosted team morale and employee satisfaction.

Reflection

AcmeCorp's journey illustrates the power of integrating DevOps with traditional ITSM to create a dynamic, agile, and customer-focused IT service delivery model. The company's success underscores the importance of cultural change, automation, and continuous improvement in achieving DevOps transformation.

Related Questions

1. What were the main challenges AcmeCorp faced before implementing DevOps?
2. How did AcmeCorp address the cultural challenges associated with integrating DevOps practices into its existing ITSM framework?
3. Which DevOps practices were most instrumental in improving AcmeCorp's deployment frequency and service stability?
4. Discuss the impact of real-time monitoring and feedback loops on AcmeCorp's service delivery and customer satisfaction.
5. What role did iterative improvements play in AcmeCorp's DevOps transformation, and how did it contribute to the overall success?

6. Reflecting on AcmeCorp's journey, what lessons can be learned about the integration of DevOps into traditional ITSM environments?
7. How did the increase in deployment frequency affect AcmeCorp's business outcomes, and what does this suggest about the value of DevOps practices?
8. In what ways did AcmeCorp's initiative to automate the delivery pipeline contribute to reducing manual errors and accelerating service delivery?

Chapter 11: Service Integration and Management (SIAM)

Introduction

Service Integration and Management, commonly known as SIAM, is a methodological approach aimed at providing a seamless, integrated suite of IT services by orchestrating the efforts of multiple service providers. This approach is becoming increasingly essential in the modern IT landscape, where organizations frequently rely on a diverse array of internal and external service providers to support their technology infrastructure. SIAM stands out as a pivotal framework, designed to ensure that all these services are delivered in a coordinated, efficient, and effective manner, thereby aligning IT service delivery with the strategic objectives of the business.

The Role of SIAM in Today's World

In today's fast-paced and complex business environment, the ability to integrate and manage multiple IT services is not just a competitive advantage but a necessity. Organizations are more dependent than ever on technology, and this reliance has led to the proliferation of specialized service providers, each contributing a piece to the overall IT puzzle. However, without a cohesive management framework like SIAM, managing these disparate services can become a source of inefficiency and friction. SIAM provides the structure needed to ensure that all services are aligned, thereby enabling organizations to achieve their business goals more effectively.

Benefits of SIAM

The benefits of implementing SIAM are manifold. Firstly, it enhances service efficiency by providing a unified view of all IT services, which helps in identifying redundancies and streamlining processes. Secondly, SIAM improves service quality by establishing consistent standards and accountability across all service providers. This unified approach facilitates better communication and collaboration, leading to more innovative and effective IT solutions. Furthermore, SIAM strengthens governance and control, enabling organizations to better manage risks and comply with regulations.

Applications of SIAM

SIAM's applications span a wide range of industries and sectors, reflecting its versatility and adaptability. From healthcare, where it can streamline patient care systems, to finance, where it ensures the reliability and security of transactions, SIAM's principles are universally applicable. In retail, SIAM can enhance the customer experience by integrating e-commerce platforms with physical logistics services seamlessly. In essence, any organization that relies on a multifaceted IT infrastructure can benefit from the SIAM approach.

SIAM's Benefits to Stakeholders

SIAM presents distinct benefits for various stakeholders, including vendors, clients, and IT departments. For vendors, SIAM offers clarity and structure in their relationships with clients, paving the way for more effective collaboration and service delivery. Clients, on the other hand, enjoy the assurance of quality and consistency across all IT services, which SIAM provides through its integrated management framework. IT departments benefit from the streamlined operations and improved governance that SIAM facilitates, enabling them to focus more on strategic initiatives rather than getting bogged down in service coordination challenges.

Real-World Examples of SIAM

One illustrative example of SIAM in action involves a global corporation that consolidated its IT services under a SIAM framework. Previously struggling with service silos and inefficiencies, the corporation implemented SIAM to integrate its diverse array of services, ranging from cloud computing to customer support. The result was a significant improvement in service delivery times, a reduction in operational costs, and an overall enhancement in customer satisfaction. Another example can be found in the public sector, where a government agency used SIAM to coordinate IT services across multiple departments, leading to improved data sharing, enhanced security, and better public service delivery.

The Role of AI in Enhancing SIAM

Artificial Intelligence (AI) holds great potential to further enhance the benefits of SIAM. Through predictive analytics, AI can anticipate service disruptions and suggest proactive measures, thereby improving service reliability. AI can also automate routine tasks, freeing up human resources to focus on more complex and strategic activities. Furthermore, AI can facilitate better decision-making in SIAM by providing insights derived from large datasets, enabling more informed choices regarding service management and integration.

Integrating Various Processes with SIAM

SIAM integrates a wide range of processes, from traditional IT service management practices like incident and change management to more strategic processes such as service design and transition. This integration ensures that all aspects of IT service delivery are aligned and managed according to a unified strategy. Additionally, SIAM can incorporate emerging processes like DevOps and agile methodologies, further enhancing the agility and responsiveness of IT services.

Managing multi-service provider models

Managing multi-service provider models is a complex yet crucial aspect of modern IT service delivery, especially in an era where businesses rely on a plethora of specialized services to meet their operational needs. This complexity is often addressed through Service Integration and Management (SIAM), which provides a structured approach to orchestrating and harmonizing the efforts of multiple service providers. The essence of managing such models lies in ensuring that despite the diversity of services, there is unity in delivery, alignment with business goals, and accountability across all parties involved.

Understanding Multi-Service Provider Models

In a multi-service provider model, an organization contracts with several external providers for different IT services. This could range from cloud computing, network infrastructure, and software development to cybersecurity, data analytics, and customer support services. Each provider brings specific expertise and capabilities to the table, but the challenge lies in managing these services cohesively to ensure they collectively support the organization's objectives.

The Significance of SIAM in Multi-Service Provider Models

SIAM plays a pivotal role in this context by acting as the integrator of these disparate services. It ensures that there is a central governance framework that defines the roles, responsibilities, and expectations from each service provider. This framework includes standardized processes for service management, consistent performance metrics, and clear communication channels, thereby facilitating a seamless service delivery mechanism that aligns with the organization's strategic goals.

Real-World Examples

Example 1: A Global Financial Institution

A global financial institution faced challenges with its IT services due to the involvement of multiple service providers, leading to inconsistent service levels and inefficiencies. By adopting a SIAM model, the institution was able to integrate these services under a unified management framework. This included establishing a centralized service desk that served as the single point of contact for all IT-related issues, regardless of which service provider was responsible. As a result, the institution saw improved service levels, better risk management, and a more agile IT infrastructure that could adapt to changing business needs.

Example 2: A Retail Chain

A large retail chain operating in multiple countries utilized a range of IT services from various providers, including e-commerce platforms, supply chain management systems, and customer relationship management (CRM) tools. The diversity of providers and the lack of coordination led to fragmented customer experiences and operational inefficiencies. By implementing a SIAM framework, the retail chain established a coherent operational model that integrated all service providers. This not only enhanced the customer experience by providing a consistent and unified interface but also improved operational efficiency by optimizing the supply chain and inventory management processes.

Benefits of Managing Multi-Service Provider Models with SIAM

1. **Improved Service Quality and Efficiency**: By ensuring all service providers work towards common service levels and objectives, SIAM enhances the overall quality and efficiency of IT services.

2. **Enhanced Agility**: A well-managed multi-service provider model allows organizations to be more agile, enabling quick adaptation to new technologies or market changes without being constrained by single-provider limitations.

3. **Risk Management**: SIAM provides a structured approach to managing risks associated with multi-service provider models, including compliance risks, operational risks, and the risk of service disruptions.

4. **Cost Optimization**: Through better coordination and the elimination of redundant services, organizations can achieve cost savings while maintaining or even improving service quality.

5. **Strategic Alignment**: Perhaps most importantly, managing multi-service provider models through SIAM ensures that IT services are always aligned with the business's strategic objectives, thereby supporting long-term success.

Best practices for service integration

Service integration, especially in the context of managing multiple IT service providers, is a critical endeavor that requires a strategic approach to ensure seamless operation, efficiency, and alignment with business objectives. Implementing best practices in service integration not only facilitates the smooth operation of services but also enhances value delivery to the organization. Here, we explore several best practices for service integration, complemented by real-world examples to illustrate their application and impact.

153

Establishing a Clear Governance Framework

Best Practice: Develop a comprehensive governance framework that outlines roles, responsibilities, decision-making authorities, and performance metrics for all service providers.

Real-World Example: A multinational corporation, facing challenges with service overlaps and inefficiencies due to the lack of a unified governance model, established a centralized governance framework for its IT services. This framework included clear guidelines on service provider responsibilities, escalation procedures, and a balanced scorecard system for performance evaluation. As a result, the corporation saw a notable improvement in service coherence and efficiency, with a 20% reduction in incident resolution times.

Implementing a Unified Service Management Platform

Best Practice: Utilize a unified IT service management (ITSM) platform that integrates service management processes across all providers, offering a single source of truth for service performance and delivery.

Real-World Example: An online retail company adopted a unified ITSM platform to integrate services from various providers, including website hosting, payment processing, and customer support. The platform enabled centralized monitoring, incident management, and analytics, leading to improved service availability and a better customer shopping experience. The company reported a 15% increase in customer satisfaction scores within six months of implementation.

Fostering Collaboration and Communication

Best Practice: Encourage regular communication and collaboration between all service providers, facilitating a culture of partnership and mutual support.

Real-World Example: A healthcare provider dealing with fragmented IT services from different vendors initiated regular cross-vendor meetings and established collaborative working groups focused on joint service improvement initiatives. This approach fostered a sense of partnership among vendors, leading to more innovative solutions for patient care technology and a 30% improvement in IT service delivery speed.

Adopting Agile and Flexible Contracts

Best Practice: Design contracts with service providers that are flexible and agile, allowing for adjustments based on evolving service requirements and business needs.

Real-World Example: A technology startup, in its early stages of growth, negotiated flexible contracts with its IT service providers, allowing for scalability and adaptability in service levels. This agility in contractual arrangements enabled the startup to rapidly scale its IT infrastructure in response to growth spurts, without being hindered by rigid service agreements.

Prioritizing Service Integration in Strategic Planning

Best Practice: Embed service integration considerations into the organization's strategic planning processes, ensuring that IT service delivery is aligned with long-term business goals.

Real-World Example: A financial services firm incorporated service integration strategies into its five-year strategic plan, with a focus on digital transformation and customer service excellence. By aligning IT service integration with these strategic objectives, the firm was able to launch a series of successful digital banking services, significantly enhancing customer engagement and market competitiveness.

Leveraging Technology for Integration

Best Practice: Utilize advanced technologies such as AI and automation to streamline service integration processes, enhance service quality, and reduce manual overhead.

Real-World Example: An international logistics company implemented AI-driven tools to automate the integration and management of its IT services, including cargo tracking systems, customer service bots, and internal communication platforms. The automation of these integration processes led to a 40% reduction in operational costs and a 25% increase in customer service response times.

Establishing Continuous Improvement Mechanisms

Best Practice: Implement mechanisms for continuous monitoring, feedback, and improvement of service integration practices, ensuring they remain effective and aligned with business needs.

Real-World Example: A government agency tasked with managing public transportation infrastructure established a continuous improvement program for its IT services, which included regular performance reviews, stakeholder surveys, and improvement workshops with service providers. This approach led to ongoing enhancements in service reliability and passenger communication systems, contributing to higher public satisfaction rates.

Conclusion

Throughout this comprehensive exploration of Service Integration and Management (SIAM) and its application in managing multi-service provider models, we've uncovered the foundational principles, strategies, and best practices that organizations can employ to navigate the complexities of modern IT service delivery. The detailed discussion provided insights into the critical role of SIAM in today's fast-evolving digital landscape, the benefits it brings to various stakeholders, and the tangible impact it has when applied effectively across diverse sectors.

From establishing a clear governance framework to fostering collaboration among service providers and leveraging advanced technologies for integration, the strategies outlined here are designed to optimize service delivery and ensure that IT services are aligned with business objectives. The real-world examples highlighted the practical application and success of these strategies in achieving enhanced efficiency, agility, and customer satisfaction.

As we conclude this chapter, it's evident that SIAM represents more than just a methodology for integrating and managing IT services. It's a strategic approach that enables organizations to harness the full potential of their IT capabilities, adapt to change, and drive continuous improvement in service delivery. By embracing the principles of SIAM, organizations can overcome the challenges associated with managing multiple service providers, mitigate risks, and capitalize on opportunities for innovation and growth.

Moreover, the discussion on the application of artificial intelligence and the detailed best practices for service integration underscore the importance of staying at the forefront of technological advancements. These tools and methodologies not only streamline the process of service integration but also pave the way for a future where IT services are more responsive, resilient, and closely aligned with the ever-changing needs of the business.

In essence, the journey through the intricacies of SIAM and service integration reveals a path towards achieving operational excellence in an era marked by digital transformation and technological convergence. For organizations looking to thrive in this environment, adopting the SIAM framework and adhering to the outlined best practices is not just a strategic choice but a necessity. By doing so, they position themselves to deliver superior service quality, foster innovation, and achieve their strategic objectives in an increasingly complex and competitive global marketplace.

Some of the questions and answers from the above chapter:

Q1: What is Service Integration and Management (SIAM)?

A1: Service Integration and Management (SIAM) is a management methodology designed to effectively integrate and manage multiple IT service providers to ensure that IT services are delivered in a coordinated, efficient, and consistent manner. It aims to align IT service delivery with the strategic objectives of the business, providing a single point of accountability for integrated services.

Q2: Why is SIAM important in today's IT environment?

A2: SIAM is crucial in today's IT environment due to the increasing reliance of organizations on a diverse array of internal and external service providers to support their technology infrastructure. SIAM addresses the challenges of managing these multiple suppliers, ensuring that all services are integrated seamlessly and delivered in alignment with the organization's business goals, thus enhancing efficiency and service quality.

Q3: What are the key benefits of implementing SIAM for an organization?

A3: The key benefits of implementing SIAM include improved efficiency and effectiveness of IT service delivery, enhanced service quality and user satisfaction, better risk management and compliance, cost optimization through elimination of redundant services, and strategic alignment between IT services and business objectives.

Q4: Can you give an example of a real-world application of SIAM?

A4: A real-world example of SIAM application can be seen in a multinational corporation that consolidated its IT services under a SIAM framework to address service overlaps and inefficiencies. By establishing a centralized governance framework and a unified IT service management platform, the corporation improved its incident resolution times by 20% and enhanced overall service delivery efficiency.

Q5: How does SIAM benefit vendors, clients, and IT departments specifically?

A5: Vendors benefit from SIAM through clearer roles and structured relationships with clients, leading to more effective service delivery. Clients enjoy consistent and high-quality IT services aligned with their business needs. IT departments gain from streamlined operations and improved governance, enabling them to focus on strategic initiatives rather than managing service providers.

Q6: What role does artificial intelligence (AI) play in enhancing SIAM?

A6: Artificial intelligence plays a significant role in enhancing SIAM by automating routine tasks, providing predictive analytics for proactive service management, and facilitating better decision-making through insights derived from data analysis. This leads to improved service reliability, efficiency, and innovation in IT service delivery.

Q7: What are some best practices for service integration in a multi-service provider model?

A7: Best practices for service integration include establishing a clear governance framework, implementing a unified service management platform, fostering collaboration and communication among service providers, adopting flexible and agile contracts, prioritizing service integration in strategic planning, leveraging technology for integration, and establishing mechanisms for continuous improvement.

Q8: What challenges might organizations face when implementing SIAM, and how can they be addressed?

A8: Challenges in implementing SIAM may include resistance to change from stakeholders, complexities in integrating services from multiple providers, and managing relationships with various vendors. These can be addressed through robust change management practices, standardizing processes and tools for integration, and establishing strong vendor management practices to ensure alignment with organizational objectives.

Q9: How does SIAM ensure that IT services are aligned with business objectives?

A9: SIAM ensures alignment with business objectives through its governance framework, which defines roles, responsibilities, and performance metrics in line with strategic goals. It facilitates regular reviews and adjustments of IT services to ensure they continue to support the organization's evolving needs and strategic direction.

Case Study: Transforming IT Service Delivery with SIAM in a Multinational Corporation

Background

A multinational corporation, operating in over 50 countries with a diverse range of IT services outsourced to multiple vendors, faced significant challenges in managing its IT service delivery. The corporation struggled with service overlaps, inefficiencies, and a lack of standardized processes across its operations, leading to increased costs and decreased service quality. To address these issues, the corporation decided to implement Service Integration and Management (SIAM) as a strategic approach to integrate and manage its IT services.

Objectives

The primary objectives of the SIAM implementation were to:

1. Streamline IT service delivery across all vendors and internal teams.

2. Improve the efficiency and effectiveness of IT services.

3. Enhance service quality and user satisfaction.

4. Achieve cost optimization through the elimination of redundant services.

5. Ensure IT services are aligned with the corporation's strategic business objectives.

Implementation

The corporation undertook a comprehensive approach to implement SIAM, which included the following key steps:

1. **Establishing a Governance Framework**: A centralized governance model was developed to define clear roles, responsibilities, and decision-making authorities for both internal and external service providers.

2. **Unified IT Service Management Platform**: The corporation implemented a unified ITSM platform that allowed for the integration of service management processes across all providers, offering a single source of truth for service performance and delivery.

3. **Fostering Collaboration and Communication**: Regular cross-vendor meetings and collaborative working groups were established to encourage a culture of partnership and mutual support among all service providers.

4. **Adopting Agile Contracts**: Contracts with service providers were redesigned to be flexible and adaptable, allowing for adjustments based on evolving service requirements and business needs.

5. **Leveraging Technology for Integration**: Advanced technologies, including AI and automation tools, were employed to streamline service integration processes and enhance service quality.

Results

Within 12 months of implementing SIAM, the corporation experienced significant improvements in its IT service delivery:

- **Improved Service Efficiency**: Incident resolution times were reduced by 20%, and overall service delivery became more efficient due to streamlined processes and reduced redundancies.

- **Enhanced Service Quality**: The unified ITSM platform and collaborative efforts led to a 15% increase in customer satisfaction scores, reflecting higher service quality and better user experiences.

- **Cost Optimization**: The corporation achieved a 25% reduction in operational costs through the elimination of redundant services and more efficient use of resources.

- **Strategic Alignment**: IT services were more closely aligned with the corporation's strategic objectives, supporting its global operations more effectively and contributing to its competitive advantage in the market.

Conclusion

The successful implementation of SIAM in this multinational corporation demonstrates the transformative potential of integrating and managing IT services in a cohesive and strategic manner. By addressing the challenges associated with managing multiple service providers and ensuring that IT services are aligned with business objectives, SIAM enabled the corporation to enhance its operational efficiency, improve service quality, and achieve significant cost savings. This case study serves as a compelling example of how SIAM can be leveraged to optimize IT service delivery and support the strategic goals of an organization in a complex and dynamic business environment.

Attempt to answer the following questions from the above case study.

1. What specific challenges did the multinational corporation face before adopting SIAM?

2. What were the primary goals set by the corporation for the SIAM implementation?

3. Which key steps were undertaken by the corporation to implement SIAM effectively?

4. How did the corporation facilitate collaboration and communication among its service providers?

5. In what ways did technology play a crucial role in the SIAM implementation process?

6. Can you list the major outcomes achieved by the corporation following SIAM implementation?

7. How did the implementation of SIAM contribute to cost optimization for the corporation?

8. Describe how SIAM implementation enhanced the strategic alignment of IT services with business objectives.

9. What were the critical success factors in the corporation's SIAM implementation?

10. What insights can other organizations gain from this corporation's experience with SIAM in a multi-vendor IT environment?

Chapter 12: Change Management for the Digital Era

Introduction

The digital era has brought about unprecedented changes in how businesses operate, compete, and thrive in a rapidly evolving landscape. With the advent of technologies such as Artificial Intelligence (AI), organizations are finding themselves at the cusp of a transformation that promises to redefine the future of work, innovation, and competitive advantage. However, this transformation is not without its challenges. To navigate the complexities of digital transformation, organizations must embrace change management principles that are tailored for the digital era. This chapter explores the integration of AI in change management, highlighting its applications, real-world examples, and the benefits it brings to organizations willing to navigate the path of digital transformation.

Applications of AI in Change Management

AI's role in change management is multifaceted, offering new ways to facilitate, accelerate, and optimize change processes. One of the primary applications of AI in change management is in predictive analytics. By analyzing vast amounts of data, AI can predict change impacts, enabling organizations to prepare and adapt strategies proactively. Additionally, AI-driven automation tools can streamline change implementation, reducing the time and resources required for routine tasks and allowing teams to focus on strategic initiatives. AI can also enhance decision-making through data-driven insights, ensuring that change initiatives are aligned with business objectives and market demands.

Real-World Examples of AI in Change Management

1. **A Global Retailer's Supply Chain Transformation**: A global retail chain utilized AI to overhaul its supply chain management. By implementing AI-driven predictive analytics, the retailer could anticipate demand fluctuations and adjust its inventory and logistics strategies accordingly. This change management initiative led to improved efficiency, reduced costs, and enhanced customer satisfaction.

2. **AI-Driven Employee Training and Development**: A multinational corporation introduced an AI-based platform to personalize employee training and development programs. The platform analyzed individual learning patterns and performance data to tailor training content, optimizing employee upskilling and reskilling efforts. This approach facilitated smoother transitions during organizational changes, enhancing workforce adaptability and engagement.

3. **Automated Customer Service Enhancement**: A telecommunications company implemented AI-powered chatbots and virtual assistants to improve its customer service. This change was part of a broader digital transformation initiative aimed at enhancing customer experience and operational efficiency. The AI-driven tools provided 24/7 customer support, significantly reducing response times and improving customer satisfaction rates.

Benefits of Change Management and AI Integration

The integration of AI into change management processes offers a plethora of benefits that can significantly enhance an organization's ability to navigate the digital transformation journey. One of the key benefits is improved efficiency. AI can automate repetitive tasks, streamline workflows, and optimize resource allocation, enabling faster and more effective change implementations. Another benefit is enhanced decision-making. AI's ability to analyze large datasets provides leaders with actionable insights, improving the quality and speed of decisions related to change initiatives. Moreover, AI-driven change management can lead to increased agility, as organizations can more swiftly adapt to market changes and technological advancements. Finally, the personalized and data-driven nature of AI can boost employee engagement and buy-in during change processes, mitigating resistance and fostering a culture of continuous improvement.

Change Management in ITIL 4

The ITIL 4 framework, which stands as the latest iteration of the IT Infrastructure Library standards, introduces a holistic approach to change management, now referred to as "Change Enablement." This shift reflects a broader perspective on change management, emphasizing the importance of enabling changes that deliver value while minimizing disruption and risks. In ITIL 4, Change Enablement is part of the Service Value System (SVS), which focuses on how organizations can co-create value through service management.

Change Enablement in ITIL 4 encourages organizations to adopt a flexible, adaptive approach to managing changes in technology and processes. It highlights the importance of understanding the nature and impact of changes, engaging stakeholders throughout the change process, and leveraging technology and data to make informed decisions. This approach is designed to support organizations in navigating the complexities of the digital era, where changes are frequent and often driven by technological advancements.

Risks of Overlooking Change Management in Technology

Failing to implement effective change management processes, especially in the context of IT services and infrastructure, can lead to significant risks:

1. **Operational Disruption**: Without a structured approach to managing changes, organizations may experience unexpected downtime or degradation of service quality, impacting business operations and customer satisfaction.

2. **Security Vulnerabilities**: Inadequately managed changes can introduce security gaps, leaving systems and data exposed to threats and breaches.

3. **Compliance Issues**: Organizations operating in regulated industries may face legal and financial penalties if changes lead to non-compliance with industry standards and regulations.

4. **Resource Wastage**: Without a clear understanding of the impact of changes, organizations may allocate resources inefficiently, leading to wasted time, effort, and financial resources.

5. **Resistance to Change**: A lack of communication and stakeholder engagement during the change process can result in resistance from employees, hindering the successful implementation of new technologies or processes.

Leveraging ITIL 4 for Effective Change Management

ITIL 4 offers several principles and practices that organizations can leverage to mitigate these risks and successfully manage changes:

- **Focus on Value**: Ensure that every change is aligned with the organization's objectives and delivers tangible benefits.

- **Start Where You Are**: Evaluate the current state of IT services and infrastructure to understand the baseline from which changes are initiated.

- **Progress Iteratively with Feedback**: Adopt an agile approach to change management, allowing for incremental improvements and adjustments based on feedback.

- **Collaborate and Promote Visibility**: Engage stakeholders across the organization in the change process, ensuring transparency and fostering a culture of collaboration.

- **Think and Work Holistically**: Consider the impact of changes on all aspects of the organization, including people, processes, technology, and partners.

- **Optimize and Automate**: Utilize technology and automation to streamline change processes, reduce manual efforts, and minimize the risk of errors.

Questions and Answers:

Q1: What is the key focus of change management in ITIL 4?

A1: The key focus of change management in ITIL 4, referred to as "Change Enablement," is to facilitate, accelerate, and optimize the process of implementing changes that deliver value to the organization while minimizing disruption and risks. It emphasizes enabling changes within the Service Value System (SVS) to support organizations in navigating the complexities of the digital era effectively.

Q2: Why is structured change management crucial in the realm of IT services and infrastructure?

A2: Structured change management is crucial in IT services and infrastructure to mitigate significant risks such as operational disruptions, security vulnerabilities, compliance issues, resource wastage, and resistance to change. Without it, organizations may face unexpected downtime, security breaches, legal penalties, inefficient resource use, and obstacles in implementing new technologies or processes.

Q3: How does ITIL 4 suggest organizations manage changes?

A3: ITIL 4 suggests that organizations manage changes by adopting a flexible, adaptive approach that includes understanding the impact of changes, engaging stakeholders, leveraging technology and data for informed decisions, and considering the holistic impact of changes on the organization. It advocates for iterative progress with feedback, collaboration, holistic thinking, and optimization through automation.

Q4: What are some of the primary risks associated with overlooking change management?

A4: Overlooking change management can lead to operational disruptions, security vulnerabilities, compliance issues, resource wastage, and resistance to change. These risks can adversely affect business operations, expose the organization to security threats, result in financial and legal penalties, and hinder the successful adoption of new processes or technologies.

Q5: What benefits does ITIL 4's Change Enablement practice offer to organizations undergoing digital transformation?

A5: ITIL 4's Change Enablement practice offers several benefits, including improved efficiency through automation, enhanced decision-making with data-driven insights, increased organizational agility to adapt to market changes, and improved employee engagement in change processes. These benefits collectively enable organizations to implement technological changes smoothly, securely, and in alignment with strategic business goals.

Q6: Describe an approach recommended by ITIL 4 for engaging stakeholders in the change process.

A6: ITIL 4 recommends engaging stakeholders in the change process through transparent communication, collaboration, and promoting visibility. This involves regular updates, feedback loops, and involving stakeholders in decision-making processes to ensure their buy-in and support throughout the change initiative. This approach fosters a culture of collaboration and mutual support, crucial for successful change implementation.

Q7: Why is automation considered important in the context of ITIL 4's change management practices?

A7: Automation is considered important in ITIL 4's change management practices because it streamlines change processes, reduces manual effort and the risk of errors, and enhances efficiency. Automation enables organizations to implement changes faster and more reliably, allowing teams to focus on strategic initiatives and ensuring a smooth transition during the change implementation phase.

Q8: How does ITIL 4 ensure that changes are aligned with organizational goals?

A8: ITIL 4 ensures that changes are aligned with organizational goals by advocating for a value-focused approach. This involves ensuring that every change is evaluated in terms of its potential to deliver tangible benefits and contribute to the organization's objectives. It also emphasizes the importance of starting from the current state, progressing iteratively with feedback, and making decisions based on comprehensive data analysis to align changes with strategic goals.

Techniques for managing organizational change

Managing organizational change, particularly in the context of the digital era where ITIL 4 and AI play pivotal roles, involves a variety of sophisticated techniques designed to ensure smooth transitions, minimize disruptions, and align technological innovations with strategic business objectives. The integration of AI into the change management processes further enriches these techniques, offering new dimensions for efficiency, predictability, and engagement. Here are some detailed techniques for managing organizational change, reflecting the insights from the discussed chapter:

1. Predictive Analytics and Data-Driven Decision Making

Utilizing AI for predictive analytics allows organizations to forecast the outcomes of proposed changes, anticipate potential challenges, and make informed decisions. This technique involves analyzing historical data, current trends, and predictive models to assess the impact of changes on various aspects of the organization, from operational processes to employee productivity. By leveraging AI-driven insights, organizations can tailor their change management strategies to mitigate risks and capitalize on opportunities, ensuring that decisions are grounded in solid data.

2. Stakeholder Engagement and Communication

Effective change management requires active engagement and clear communication with all stakeholders, including employees, management, vendors, and customers. Techniques such as targeted communication campaigns, workshops, and feedback sessions are vital. AI tools can enhance these efforts by analyzing communication effectiveness, sentiment analysis, and identifying stakeholders' concerns in real-time. By adopting a proactive approach to address queries and concerns, organizations can build trust, reduce resistance, and foster a culture that embraces change.

3. Agile and Iterative Approach

Adopting an agile and iterative approach to change management, as emphasized in ITIL 4, allows organizations to implement changes in manageable increments. This technique enables continuous assessment and adaptation of strategies based on feedback and outcomes. Agile methodologies, supported by AI for task automation and workflow optimization, ensure that change processes are flexible and responsive to emerging challenges and opportunities.

4. Training and Upskilling Initiatives

To navigate the complexities of digital transformation, organizations must invest in training and upskilling initiatives for their workforce. Leveraging AI-driven platforms can personalize learning experiences, identify skill gaps, and monitor progress, making training more effective and aligned with the needs of both the organization and its employees. This technique ensures that the workforce is prepared and equipped to adapt to new technologies and processes introduced by change initiatives.

5. Change Impact Analysis and Planning

Before implementing any change, conducting a thorough change impact analysis is crucial. This involves evaluating the potential effects of change on different areas of the organization, including IT infrastructure, business processes, and employee roles. AI can assist in this process by providing comprehensive analyses of vast amounts of data to predict outcomes and identify potential areas of concern. With this information, organizations can develop detailed change plans that address identified risks and outline clear steps for implementation.

6. Monitoring and Continuous Improvement

Post-implementation monitoring and continuous improvement are essential for sustaining the benefits of change initiatives. Techniques include setting up KPIs (Key Performance Indicators) and using AI tools to track performance, analyze feedback, and identify areas for refinement. Continuous monitoring allows organizations to quickly address any issues that arise and make adjustments to enhance the effectiveness of changes, ensuring ongoing alignment with business goals.

7. Building a Culture of Change

Finally, fostering an organizational culture that is open to change is fundamental. Techniques for achieving this include recognizing and rewarding flexibility and innovation, creating opportunities for employee involvement in change initiatives, and promoting transparency throughout the change process. AI can support these efforts by identifying patterns in employee engagement and pinpointing areas where additional support or communication is needed.

In conclusion, managing organizational change in the digital era requires a blend of traditional change management techniques and innovative approaches enabled by AI and ITIL 4 principles. By leveraging predictive analytics, engaging stakeholders effectively, adopting an agile approach, investing in training, conducting thorough planning, and fostering a culture open to change, organizations can navigate the complexities of digital transformation successfully. These techniques, underpinned by data-driven insights and automated processes, not only facilitate smoother transitions but also ensure that changes deliver lasting value to the organization.

Building a culture of continuous improvement

Building a culture of continuous improvement is a critical facet of managing organizational change, especially in the digital era where technologies like AI and frameworks like ITIL 4 significantly influence how changes are implemented and managed. This culture is pivotal not only for the success of individual change initiatives but also for ensuring the long-term adaptability and competitiveness of an organization. Here's a detailed exploration of how a culture of continuous improvement can be cultivated, drawing on principles from the discussed chapter on change management in the digital era.

Embracing the Principles of ITIL 4 and AI

A culture of continuous improvement is deeply rooted in the principles of ITIL 4, which emphasizes the importance of iterative progress, feedback, and the continuous alignment of IT services with business needs. Integrating AI into this process enhances the capability to analyze data, predict outcomes, and automate repetitive tasks, thereby fostering an environment where improvement is constant, and innovation is encouraged.

Fostering an Agile Mindset

An agile mindset is essential for continuous improvement. It encourages flexibility, responsiveness to change, and the willingness to experiment and learn from failures. By adopting agile methodologies, organizations can implement changes in smaller, manageable increments, allowing for regular assessment and adjustment based on feedback and performance data. This approach, supported by AI-driven insights, ensures that strategies remain relevant and effective over time.

Encouraging Collaboration and Open Communication

Building a culture of continuous improvement requires open lines of communication and collaboration across all levels of the organization. Encouraging the sharing of ideas, successes, and failures creates a supportive environment where employees feel valued and engaged in the process of improvement. Leveraging AI tools for sentiment analysis and communication effectiveness can help identify areas where further encouragement or support is needed to foster a collaborative culture.

Leveraging Data for Insights and Decision Making

Data is at the heart of continuous improvement, especially in the digital era. Utilizing AI to analyze performance metrics, customer feedback, and operational data provides valuable insights that can drive improvement initiatives. By making data-driven decisions, organizations can ensure that their efforts are focused on areas that offer the greatest impact on performance and customer satisfaction.

Investing in Training and Development

Continuous improvement also depends on the skills and knowledge of the workforce. Investing in ongoing training and development, particularly in areas related to AI and digital technologies, ensures that employees are equipped to contribute effectively to improvement initiatives. AI-driven learning platforms can personalize training programs to meet the specific needs of individuals, enhancing their ability to adapt to and drive change.

Implementing a Systematic Approach to Improvement

Adopting a systematic approach to continuous improvement, such as the Plan-Do-Check-Act (PDCA) cycle, helps organizations structure their improvement efforts. This approach involves planning changes based on data-driven insights, implementing changes in a controlled manner, checking the results against expected outcomes, and acting on what has been learned to make further improvements. AI can facilitate this process by providing accurate data analysis and automating aspects of the implementation and monitoring phases.

Recognizing and Rewarding Improvement Efforts

Recognizing and rewarding the efforts of teams and individuals who contribute to continuous improvement is crucial for sustaining motivation and engagement. Establishing recognition programs that highlight successes in innovation and improvement can reinforce the value placed on these efforts. AI tools can assist in tracking contributions and outcomes, ensuring that recognition is based on measurable achievements.

Conclusion

In conclusion, navigating the complexities of organizational change in the digital era demands a nuanced approach, blending traditional change management principles with the innovative capabilities offered by AI and the structured guidance of ITIL 4. This chapter has explored the pivotal role of AI in enhancing change management processes, offering predictive insights, automating routine tasks, and fostering a culture of continuous improvement. The application of ITIL 4 principles further enriches this approach by emphasizing agility, stakeholder engagement, and the iterative refinement of strategies to align IT services with business objectives effectively.

The detailed exploration of techniques for managing organizational change underscores the necessity of an adaptive, data-driven approach. From leveraging predictive analytics and fostering open communication to implementing a systematic approach to improvement, these strategies collectively enable organizations to respond to the digital era's challenges with agility and resilience. The emphasis on building a culture of continuous improvement is particularly significant, as it encapsulates the essence of what it means to thrive in a constantly evolving landscape. Such a culture not only supports the successful implementation of specific change initiatives but also ensures the long-term sustainability and competitiveness of the organization.

Through real-world examples and a discussion of the benefits associated with integrating AI and adhering to ITIL 4 practices, this chapter has illuminated the path forward for organizations seeking to navigate digital transformation successfully. The key takeaway is that change management in the digital era is not just about implementing new technologies or processes; it's about fostering an organizational culture that embraces change, values continuous improvement, and leverages data and technology to drive decision-making and innovation.

As organizations continue to confront the rapid pace of technological advancement, the principles and practices outlined in this chapter provide a roadmap for managing change effectively. By embracing the synergies between AI, ITIL 4, and a culture of continuous improvement, organizations can navigate the digital era's challenges with confidence, ensuring that they not only survive but thrive in the face of change.

Following are the questions and answers of the above chapter

Q1: How does AI enhance change management processes in the digital era?

A1: AI enhances change management processes by offering predictive insights, automating routine tasks, and enabling data-driven decision-making. It improves efficiency, reduces manual errors, and provides organizations with the ability to forecast the outcomes of change initiatives, ensuring a more strategic and informed approach to managing change.

Q2: What role do ITIL 4 principles play in managing organizational change?

A2: ITIL 4 principles play a crucial role in managing organizational change by emphasizing agility, stakeholder engagement, and the iterative refinement of strategies. These principles guide organizations in aligning IT services with business objectives, facilitating flexible and responsive change management processes that can adapt to the evolving needs of the digital era.

Q3: Why is building a culture of continuous improvement important in organizational change management?

A3: Building a culture of continuous improvement is important because it fosters an environment where employees are encouraged to seek out, propose, and implement improvements. This culture supports the successful implementation of change initiatives and ensures long-term organizational sustainability and competitiveness by constantly adapting to changes and optimizing processes.

Q4: How can organizations leverage predictive analytics in change management?

A4: Organizations can leverage predictive analytics in change management by using AI to analyze historical data, current trends, and predictive models. This allows them to anticipate potential challenges, forecast the impacts of proposed changes, and tailor their strategies to mitigate risks and capitalize on opportunities, leading to more successful change initiatives.

Q5: What are the benefits of adopting an agile and iterative approach to change management?

A5: The benefits of adopting an agile and iterative approach to change management include enhanced flexibility, the ability to respond quickly to feedback and changes in the environment, and the reduction of risks associated with large-scale changes. This approach allows for continuous assessment and adaptation of strategies, ensuring that change initiatives remain aligned with organizational goals.

Q6: How does AI support systematic approaches to continuous improvement, such as the Plan-Do-Check-Act (PDCA) cycle?

A6: AI supports systematic approaches to continuous improvement by providing accurate data analysis for planning, automating aspects of the implementation (Do) phase, offering real-time monitoring tools for the Check phase, and analyzing outcomes to inform further action. This enhances the effectiveness of the PDCA cycle, enabling more precise and efficient continuous improvement efforts.

Q7: What strategies can organizations use to foster open communication and collaboration during change initiatives?

A7: Organizations can foster open communication and collaboration by utilizing AI tools for sentiment analysis, establishing regular cross-functional meetings, creating collaborative platforms for idea sharing, and ensuring transparency throughout the change process. Engaging stakeholders through clear, targeted communication campaigns and feedback mechanisms also encourages participation and buy-in.

Q8: In what ways do training and development initiatives support change management in the digital era?

A8: Training and development initiatives support change management by equipping employees with the necessary skills and knowledge to adapt to new technologies and processes. AI-driven learning platforms can personalize training to meet individual needs, enhancing the effectiveness of upskilling efforts and ensuring that the workforce is prepared to contribute to the organization's change initiatives.

Case Study

Background

TechGlobal Inc., a leading software development company, faced significant challenges in adapting to the rapidly evolving technology landscape. The company recognized the need for a comprehensive digital transformation to enhance its product offerings, improve operational efficiency, and maintain a competitive edge. However, the management was aware that such a transformation would require a fundamental change in how the organization managed and implemented change initiatives.

Objective

TechGlobal Inc. aimed to integrate Artificial Intelligence (AI) and adhere to ITIL 4 principles to streamline its change management processes. The objectives were to improve predictive insights, automate routine tasks, foster a culture of continuous improvement, and ensure that the digital transformation aligned with the company's strategic business objectives.

Implementation

1. Leveraging AI for Predictive Analytics and Automation: TechGlobal Inc. implemented AI-driven tools to forecast the outcomes of proposed changes and automate repetitive tasks. This enabled the company to anticipate potential challenges and optimize resource allocation.

2. Adopting ITIL 4 Principles: The company adopted ITIL 4 principles to guide its change management process. This included focusing on value, starting where they are, progressing iteratively with feedback, and collaborating and promoting visibility.

3. Building a Culture of Continuous Improvement: TechGlobal Inc. emphasized the importance of continuous improvement by encouraging employees to identify and implement improvement opportunities. AI-driven platforms were used to

track performance and facilitate personalized training programs.

4. Engaging Stakeholders: The company established regular communication channels and feedback mechanisms to ensure transparency and engage stakeholders throughout the change process.

Results

Six months after implementing these strategies, TechGlobal Inc. reported significant improvements:

- Enhanced Efficiency: Predictive analytics and automation reduced the time to market for new product features by 30%.

- Improved Decision-Making: Data-driven insights enabled the company to make more strategic decisions regarding its digital transformation initiatives.

- Increased Agility: The agile and iterative approach allowed TechGlobal Inc. to quickly adapt to changes in the technology landscape, ensuring that its products remained competitive.

- Higher Employee Engagement: The culture of continuous improvement led to a 40% increase in employee-initiated improvement projects.

Conclusion

TechGlobal Inc.'s experience highlights the effectiveness of integrating AI and ITIL 4 principles into change management processes. By leveraging technology to enhance predictive insights, automate tasks, and foster a culture of continuous improvement, the company successfully navigated its digital transformation. This case study demonstrates that a strategic approach to change management, grounded in data-driven decision-making and stakeholder engagement, can significantly enhance an organization's ability to adapt to the digital era.

Related Questions and Answers

Q1: How did TechGlobal Inc. use AI to enhance its change management process?

Q2: What ITIL 4 principles did TechGlobal Inc. adopt, and why?

Q3: What were the outcomes of implementing AI and ITIL 4 principles at TechGlobal Inc.?

Q4: How did building a culture of continuous improvement impact TechGlobal Inc.?

Chapter 13: Leadership in Technology: Beyond Management

Visionary Leadership for IT

Introduction

In the ever-evolving landscape of information technology, the difference between a good organization and a great one often hinges on leadership. While management is about handling the present, leadership is about creating the future. Visionary leadership in IT is not confined to maintaining systems and processes; it extends to leading with an imaginative foresight that aligns technology with business imperatives, propelling an organization towards its long-term aspirations.

The Essence of Visionary Leadership

Visionary IT leaders possess an intrinsic ability to look beyond the horizon. They are not just the custodians of current technology but are also the architects of the future. These leaders recognize that IT is a pivotal force in shaping business strategies and driving change. Their approach is characterized by several key elements:

- Strategic Insight: Visionary leaders are adept at interpreting market trends and technological advancements, integrating this knowledge into strategic planning to ensure their organization remains ahead of the curve.

- Innovative Mindset: They foster a culture of innovation where new ideas are valued and explored. This means not only keeping abreast of emerging technologies but also understanding their potential impact on the business.

- Adaptive Strategy: In an age where change is the only constant, these leaders excel in agility and adaptability, aligning IT strategies with dynamic business needs and thereby ensuring resilience and relevance.

- Influential Communication: They have a compelling way of articulating their vision, convincing stakeholders of the value of investing in new technologies and inspiring their teams to turn vision into reality.

Real-World Cases

Several organizations exemplify visionary leadership in IT. For instance:

- A major retail company implemented an AI-based system to personalize customer experience, predicting buying habits and suggesting products, leading to a significant increase in sales.

- A global logistics firm utilized IoT technology to optimize their supply chain, resulting in enhanced visibility, improved efficiency, and reduced operational costs.

- A financial services provider adopted blockchain technology to secure transactions and simplify processes, thereby gaining a competitive edge in the market.

These cases demonstrate how visionary IT leaders are not just enhancing their existing services but are transforming the way their industries operate.

Visionary Leadership and ITIL 4

ITIL 4, with its focus on managing IT as a service, provides a comprehensive framework for IT leaders to align their vision with practical execution. It emphasizes the co-creation of value through service relationships, encouraging leaders to think beyond traditional IT metrics and towards broader business outcomes.

- Focus on Value: Visionary leaders align IT initiatives with the creation of value as defined collaboratively with stakeholders, ensuring that every technological investment has a clear purpose and measurable impact.

- Holistic Approach: ITIL 4 encourages a holistic approach to service management. Visionary leaders take into account the four dimensions of service management: organizations and people, information and technology, partners and suppliers, and value streams and processes.

- Iterative Progress: With the guidance of the ITIL 4 framework, leaders adopt an iterative approach to project management and service delivery, enabling the organization to respond to change efficiently and effectively.

- Guiding Principles: ITIL 4's seven guiding principles (such as 'start where you are', 'progress iteratively with feedback', and 'keep it simple and practical') act as beacons for visionary leaders, guiding decision-making and strategy formulation.

Visionary Leadership for IT

Visionary leadership within the realm of IT is more crucial than ever in the age of rapid technological evolution and digital transformation. Unlike traditional management, which often focuses on maintaining the status quo and managing resources efficiently, visionary leadership is about setting a strategic direction that can harness the potential of technology to create new value.

Visionary IT leaders are far-sighted, seeing beyond the current technological landscape to the horizon of possibilities. They understand that technology is not an end in itself but a means to achieve broader business objectives. These leaders anticipate the impact of technological advancements and align their IT strategy with the future needs of the business, ensuring that the organization is agile and adaptable in the face of change.

One of the essential elements of visionary leadership in IT is the ability to forecast future trends. This doesn't merely involve keeping up with the latest technological innovations but also involves understanding how these innovations can disrupt or enhance business models and processes. Visionary IT leaders are adept at reading the market, understanding customer expectations, and leveraging emerging technologies to meet those needs more effectively.

For instance, a visionary IT leader might recognize the potential of AI and machine learning to not just streamline operations but also to create entirely new customer experiences, leading to the development of predictive service models that anticipate and solve customer problems before they occur. By staying attuned to the pulse of technological progress, these leaders can guide their organizations through digital transformation initiatives that deliver real business results.

In the context of ITIL 4, visionary leadership aligns well with the framework's focus on co-creating business value through service management. ITIL 4 emphasizes the importance of understanding the stakeholder's needs and ensuring that the IT organization's work is fully aligned with the value streams and processes that facilitate business objectives. A visionary IT leader, therefore, is someone who embodies the ITIL 4 principles by continuously seeking ways to improve and innovate service management practices in alignment with the evolving business environment.

Building and Leading High-Performance Teams

Building and leading high-performance teams in the IT sector is about much more than technical expertise. It requires creating a culture of excellence, where team members are motivated, engaged, and united in their pursuit of the organization's goals.

High-performance teams in IT are composed of individuals with diverse skills and backgrounds. These teams are characterized by a high level of collaboration and are able to leverage their collective knowledge to solve complex problems and innovate. The role of the leader is to ensure that this diversity translates into strength rather than discord.

Leaders of high-performance teams set clear goals and create an environment where team members understand their roles and how their work contributes to the larger objectives. They

188

foster a culture of accountability and empowerment, where team members feel confident to take initiative and make decisions within their areas of expertise. This empowerment is balanced with a clear framework of expectations and performance metrics to ensure that everyone is moving in the same direction.

Effective leaders also prioritize communication, ensuring that team members are not only informed about what is happening within the team and the broader organization but also feel heard. They encourage open dialogue, constructive feedback, and the sharing of ideas. This openness promotes a culture of continuous learning and improvement, which is essential in the ever-changing field of IT.

Moreover, leaders of high-performance teams understand the importance of recognition and reward. They acknowledge individual and team achievements, which not only boosts morale but also reinforces the behaviors and outcomes that lead to success.

In line with the principles of ITIL 4, building and leading high-performance teams involves a focus on collaboration, transparency, and a commitment to ongoing development. These teams are regularly engaged with stakeholders and are integral to the continual improvement process, ensuring that the IT services they deliver are always aligned with changing business needs and are contributing maximum value.

Conclusion

In the evolving landscape of information technology, leadership transcends the confines of traditional management. Visionary leadership for IT demands a blend of foresight, innovation, and a deep understanding of the transformative role technology plays in driving business success. Visionary leaders are the architects of tomorrow's IT strategies, anticipating future trends and guiding their organizations through the uncharted territories of digital transformation. They are not merely reactive to change; they are proactive, strategic, and always aligned with the broader objectives of the organization.

Moreover, the ability to cultivate and steer high-performance teams stands as a testament to the efficacy of such leadership. These teams, formed from diverse talents and a collaborative culture, are the engines of innovation and excellence. A visionary leader not only inspires individual achievement but synergizes these efforts towards collective success. In the light of ITIL 4, these leaders and teams are not just supporting the business; they are integral to its very fabric, co-creating value and ensuring agility and resilience in a competitive environment.

In conclusion, as we forge ahead in this digital era, the distinction between managing and leading becomes increasingly significant. The impact of a visionary leader coupled with a high-performance team is profound, resonating through the enhanced capabilities of IT service management, the achievement of strategic goals, and the realization of a shared vision. This is the essence of leadership in technology: to go beyond the routine of management, to inspire, to innovate, and to lead with conviction towards a future where technology and human ingenuity are interwoven to drive progress and prosperity.

Following are the questions and answers from the above chapter.

Q1: How do you define visionary leadership in the context of IT, and how does it differ from traditional IT management?

A1: Visionary leadership in IT is about setting a strategic direction that leverages technology for business innovation and growth, rather than just maintaining and optimizing current systems. Unlike traditional IT management, which often focuses on efficiency and stability, visionary leadership requires a forward-looking approach that embraces change, anticipates future trends, and prepares the organization for new challenges and opportunities. It involves understanding the transformative potential of technology and aligning IT initiatives with the long-term goals of the organization.

Q2: Can you provide an example of a time when you anticipated a significant technology trend and successfully positioned the organization to capitalize on it?

A2: Speak to a specific instance, such as the early adoption of cloud services, the implementation of AI and machine learning, or the introduction of a cybersecurity framework that anticipated regulatory changes.

Q3: How do you foster innovation within your IT department and across the organization?

A3: Innovation is fostered by creating an environment that encourages experimentation and learning from failure. We implement programs that allow employees to work on passion projects and invest in continuous learning opportunities. Regular hackathons or idea incubators can also be platforms where team members can propose and prototype new solutions, with the best ideas being integrated into our IT strategy.

Q4: In your view, what are the key characteristics of a high-performance IT team?

A4: A high-performance IT team is diverse, agile, and collaborative. Key characteristics include a clear understanding of strategic goals, well-defined roles, and responsibilities that leverage each member's strengths, a strong sense of accountability, and a commitment to continuous improvement. Effective communication and the ability to respond rapidly to change are also vital traits.

Q5: Describe a strategy you have used to build a high-performance team.

A5: Building a high-performance team involves careful selection of team members for both technical skills and cultural fit, clear communication of goals and expectations, and fostering a sense of ownership and empowerment. Regular training and team-building exercises ensure skills are sharp and the team is cohesive. I also ensure that there are clear metrics in place to measure performance and regular check-ins to keep everyone aligned and motivated.

Q6: How do you ensure that your IT strategy is aligned with the broader business objectives?

A6: Alignment is achieved through regular communication with other business leaders to understand their challenges and objectives. IT strategy is then developed not in isolation but as an integral part of the business strategy, ensuring that technology initiatives support and drive business goals. We also utilize frameworks like ITIL 4 to integrate IT services with business needs effectively.

Q7: What role does ITIL 4 play in your approach to visionary leadership and team building?

A7: ITIL 4 plays a pivotal role by providing a comprehensive framework for aligning IT service management with business needs. Its focus on co-creating business value, optimizing risk, and improving stakeholder relationships is integral to my approach to leadership. It ensures that our IT initiatives are always in service of the organization's objectives and that our teams are working on projects that have a meaningful impact.

Q8: How do you balance the need for innovation with the risk that comes with implementing new technologies?

A8: Balancing innovation with risk involves a calculated approach where potential benefits are weighed against the risks. We conduct thorough risk assessments, pilot programs, and proof-of-concept studies before full-scale implementation. It's also about creating a culture that understands the value of both innovation and risk management, ensuring that we are making informed decisions that can drive the business forward without exposing it to undue harm.

Q9: What metrics do you use to measure the performance of your IT teams, and how do you ensure these metrics drive the right behavior?

A9: We measure performance based on a balanced scorecard that includes both quantitative and qualitative metrics, such as project delivery times, budget adherence, system uptime, user satisfaction scores, and the rate of innovation. These metrics are aligned with our business objectives to ensure that they drive behaviors that contribute to the organization's success.

Q10: How do you lead your teams through periods of significant change or transformation?

A10: Leading through change involves clear and transparent communication about the reasons for the change and the benefits it will bring. It's important to involve the team in the change process, listening to their input and addressing their concerns. Providing training and support helps ease the transition, and celebrating milestones and successes reinforces the positive aspects of the change.

Case Study: Visionary Leadership and High-Performance Teams at TechGlobal Corp

Background

TechGlobal Corp, a multinational organization specializing in fintech solutions, faced the challenge of staying ahead in a highly competitive market characterized by rapid technological change. The CIO, Alex Renner, recognized the need to transform the IT department from a traditional support function into a strategic partner that could drive business innovation and growth.

Situation

The company had several legacy systems that were costly to maintain and unable to meet the agility required for new fintech products. The IT team was siloed, with low morale and a lack of clear direction. Renner was tasked with overhauling the IT strategy to support a move towards digital banking solutions while also building a high-performance team capable of executing this vision.

Action

Renner took a two-pronged approach:

1. **Visionary Leadership for IT:**

     - **Strategic IT Roadmap:** Renner developed a 5-year IT roadmap aligned with the company's goal to become a leader in digital banking solutions.

     - **Forecasting Trends:** He invested in AI and blockchain research, anticipating these technologies' pivotal roles in fintech's future.

- **Innovation Culture:** Renner introduced an 'Innovation Lab' where IT staff could work on emerging technologies and potential fintech products.

2. **Building High-Performance Teams:**

   - **Reorganization:** Renner restructured the IT department to break down silos, creating cross-functional teams focused on different aspects of the digital banking strategy.

   - **Skill Development:** He launched a comprehensive training program to upskill employees in cloud computing, AI, and agile methodologies.

   - **Performance Metrics:** Renner defined new KPIs focused on project delivery, innovation, and customer satisfaction.

Results

- **Business Alignment:** The IT roadmap successfully aligned with business objectives, leading to several successful digital banking products.

- **Innovation Output:** The Innovation Lab became a hub for breakthrough ideas, with two patents filed in the first year.

- **Team Performance:** The restructured teams showed increased productivity and improved morale. Employee retention rates went up by 15%.

- **Customer Satisfaction:** Surveys showed a 25% increase in customer satisfaction due to improved digital services.

Based on your reading of the above case study, try answering the following questions:

Q1: How did you determine which technology trends to focus on for your IT roadmap?

Q2: Can you describe the process of introducing and fostering an innovation culture in your IT department?

Q3: What specific actions did you take to reorganize the IT department, and how did you ensure these actions would lead to the creation of high-performance teams?

Q4: How did you develop the new KPIs for your IT teams, and what impact did these have on team behaviors and outcomes?

Q5: What challenges did you encounter while leading your teams through this transformation, and how did you address them?

Q6: How did you measure the success of the Innovation Lab, and what were some key learnings from its implementation?

Q7: In retrospect, what would you have done differently in your approach to achieving a high-performance IT team?

Q8: How did the ITIL 4 framework influence your strategy, especially concerning team performance and innovation?

Q9: How did you balance the risks and benefits of investing in emerging technologies like AI and blockchain?

Q10: How do you plan to sustain and build upon the successes of your IT transformation initiative in the coming years?

Chapter 14: Fostering Innovation and Creativity

Introduction

In the rapidly evolving world of information technology, fostering innovation and creativity is not just an advantage—it's a necessity. An innovative IT organization is one that consistently stays ahead of the curve, not only in adopting new technologies but also in pioneering them. This chapter delves into the mechanisms of cultivating an environment that breeds innovation and the strategies to encourage creative problem-solving within IT teams. It aligns these concepts with the ITIL 4 framework, ensuring that creativity is not a standalone effort but an integral part of service management that adds value to the entire organization.

Cultivating an Innovative IT Organization

An innovative IT organization is characterized by its ability to generate new ideas and transform them into value-creating services and products. This requires a culture that promotes risk-taking, rewards ingenuity, and learns from failure.

Real-World Example: Google, known for its innovative culture, has historically allowed its engineers to spend 20% of their time on projects that interest them, which has led to the creation of products like Gmail and AdSense. This approach aligns with ITIL 4's principle of "Start where you are," leveraging existing talents and interests to foster innovation.

Strategies for Cultivating Innovation:

1. **Empowerment:** Giving IT staff the autonomy to explore new ideas and the authority to make decisions related to their work encourages a sense of ownership and a willingness to innovate.

2. **Diverse Teams:** Bringing together individuals with different backgrounds and skill sets can spark creativity as they are likely to approach problems from various perspectives.

3. **Collaborative Environment:** A collaborative culture supported by tools that facilitate communication and idea sharing is essential. Tools like innovation hubs or internal social networks can be used.

4. **Innovation Labs:** Establishing dedicated spaces or labs where employees can work on creative projects without the pressure of day-to-day tasks can lead to breakthroughs in technology and process improvements.

5. **Recognition and Rewards:** Acknowledging and rewarding innovation reinforces the behavior and motivates others to think outside the box.

Encouraging Creative Problem-Solving

Creative problem-solving in IT means looking beyond conventional solutions to challenges. It involves questioning the status quo and considering multiple perspectives to arrive at effective solutions.

Real-World Example: Apple's creation of the iPhone was a result of creative problem-solving. The company didn't just improve an existing product; they reimagined the mobile phone as a multi-purpose device, integrating phone, music player, and internet communicator into one.

Strategies for Creative Problem-Solving:

1. **Design Thinking:** Adopting a design thinking approach to problem-solving encourages empathy with users, which can lead to more innovative and user-centric IT services.

2. **Brainstorming Sessions:** Regularly scheduled brainstorming sessions where all ideas are welcomed and no criticism is allowed can help in uncovering unique solutions.

3. **Cross-Functional Collaboration:** Inviting members from different departments to participate in problem-solving

can introduce new insights and broaden the range of potential solutions.

4. **Learning from Other Industries:** Sometimes the best creative solutions come from looking at how other industries solve their problems and adapting those solutions to the IT context.

5. **Prototyping:** Encouraging the development of prototypes and proofs of concept to test out ideas can help refine them into workable solutions.

ITIL 4 and Creativity

ITIL 4 places a strong emphasis on the co-creation of value and the continual improvement of services. This aligns perfectly with the need for innovation and creativity within IT organizations.

Scenarios for Applying ITIL 4 Concepts:

- **Value Stream Mapping:** By mapping out value streams, IT teams can identify areas ripe for innovation and streamline processes to maximize value creation.

- **Continual Improvement Model:** This model provides a structured approach to identify and implement creative improvements in service management practices.

- **Guiding Principles:** Principles such as "Focus on value," "Think and work holistically," and "Keep it simple and practical" guide IT teams to seek out innovative and creative solutions that have a real impact.

Cultivating an Innovative IT Organization

Introduction

In the context of ITIL 4, cultivating an innovative IT organization involves much more than simply adopting new technologies or implementing change. It's about fostering a culture that systematically nurtures innovation as a core value and operationalizes creativity within every process and service. ITIL 4's service value system (SVS) provides a robust framework that enables organizations to effectively align their innovative efforts with their overall service management practices.

Embedding Innovation in Culture

An innovative IT organization is one that embeds the practice of innovation into its very culture. This means going beyond ad hoc creative initiatives to developing an environment where innovation is part of the everyday workflow. ITIL 4 emphasizes a holistic approach to service management, recognizing that innovative ideas can come from any part of the organization. To this end, leadership must be committed to creating an atmosphere where innovative thinking is expected, encouraged, and rewarded.

Real-World Example: Amazon's leadership principle of "Invent and Simplify" encourages employees to seek out new ideas and reduce complexities, which has led to innovations such as AWS and Amazon Go stores. This principle aligns with ITIL 4's drive for simplification and efficiency within service management.

Strategies for Fostering Innovation:

1. **Continuous Learning:** Encourage a culture of continuous learning and exploration. ITIL 4's Continual Improvement Model can be applied not just for process improvement but also for encouraging the acquisition of new skills and knowledge, which is foundational for innovation.

2. **Diverse Collaborative Teams:** Cultivate diverse teams with varied expertise and encourage collaboration. This diversity is key in providing a range of perspectives and skills, which ITIL 4 recognizes as essential for delivering comprehensive and innovative services.

3. **Innovation Metrics:** Develop metrics to measure innovation as part of service delivery and management. ITIL 4's focus on measurement and reporting can be expanded to include innovation metrics, ensuring that creative efforts are tracked and recognized.

4. **Innovation Sprints:** Organize regular innovation sprints or hackathons, where teams can focus solely on developing new ideas or solutions. ITIL 4 supports this through the 'Plan-Do-Check-Act' model, which can be used to structure these events.

Encouraging Creative Problem-Solving

Introduction

Creative problem-solving in ITIL 4 involves utilizing the framework's principles to approach challenges in novel and effective ways. ITIL 4 encourages organizations to look beyond traditional solutions, fostering a mindset that views problems as opportunities for improvement and innovation.

Leveraging ITIL 4 for Creative Solutions

ITIL 4's principle of "Start where you are" and "Progress iteratively with feedback" are especially relevant when tackling complex IT challenges. By assessing the current state and making incremental improvements based on feedback, IT teams can creatively enhance services without the need for wholesale changes that may disrupt service delivery.

Real-World Example: Spotify's model of autonomous "squads" focuses on small, cross-functional teams responsible for specific features or services. This model facilitates creative problem-solving by empowering teams to iterate rapidly and receive immediate feedback. This approach is in line with ITIL 4's guidance on working holistically and being agile.

Strategies for Creative Problem-Solving:

1. **Design Thinking Workshops:** Employ design thinking techniques in workshops to empathize with users and redefine problems, which is supported by ITIL 4's focus on co-creating value with stakeholders.

2. **Idea Management Systems:** Implement systems to manage and track ideas from inception through to realization, echoing ITIL 4's 'Information and Technology' management practice, which supports the organization's information flows and decision-making.

3. **Cross-Domain Collaboration:** Facilitate collaboration between IT and other business domains to solve problems more creatively, a practice that resonates with ITIL 4's holistic view of service management.

By integrating these strategies with the ITIL 4 framework, IT organizations can enhance their creative problem-solving capabilities, leading to services that not only meet customer needs but also inspire delight and drive engagement.

Conclusion

In conclusion, the journey towards cultivating an innovative IT organization and encouraging creative problem-solving is both challenging and rewarding. It requires a fundamental shift in culture, mindset, and practices that aligns closely with the principles and guidelines provided by ITIL 4. By embedding innovation into the culture and operationalizing creativity within every process and service, organizations can harness the full potential of their IT capabilities to drive business success.

The strategies outlined for fostering innovation and creative problem-solving are not just theoretical ideals but practical steps that can be implemented within the ITIL 4 framework. From continuous learning and diverse collaborative teams to innovation metrics and design thinking workshops, these strategies offer a roadmap for IT organizations seeking to differentiate themselves in a competitive landscape.

Real-world examples from companies like Amazon and Spotify demonstrate the tangible benefits of adopting these approaches. They serve as a testament to the power of innovation and creativity in achieving operational excellence and delivering exceptional value to customers.

As we move forward in an era defined by rapid technological advancement and complex challenges, the principles of ITIL 4 provide a solid foundation for organizations aiming to stay ahead of the curve. By embracing the ethos of continual improvement, fostering a culture of innovation, and encouraging creative problem-solving, IT organizations can not only adapt to the changing landscape but also become catalysts for transformation and growth within their broader enterprises.

In essence, the journey of fostering innovation and creativity within IT is an ongoing process of learning, experimenting, and evolving. It is about making innovation and creativity integral to the way IT services are managed and delivered, thereby ensuring that the organization remains resilient, agile, and capable of leading the way in the digital age.

Following are the questions and answers based on the above chapter:

Q1: How can an IT organization cultivate an environment that fosters innovation according to ITIL 4?
A1: An IT organization can cultivate an innovative environment by adopting ITIL 4 practices such as fostering a culture of continuous learning, encouraging experimentation, leveraging Agile and Lean methodologies for quick iterations, and utilizing the Guiding Principles of ITIL 4, such as "Start where you are" and "Keep it simple and practical," to encourage innovative thinking and problem-solving.

Q2: Give an example of a company that has successfully cultivated an innovative IT organization.
A2: Google is a prime example, with its 20% project time policy that allows employees to spend 20% of their time on projects they are passionate about, which has led to innovations like Gmail and AdSense. This approach echoes ITIL 4's emphasis on creating a culture that encourages innovation and continuous improvement.

Q3: What strategies can IT leaders employ to encourage creative problem-solving within their teams?
A3: IT leaders can encourage creative problem-solving by promoting a psychologically safe environment where team members feel comfortable sharing ideas without fear of judgment, implementing brainstorming sessions, providing access to continuous learning resources, and rewarding innovative solutions. These practices are aligned with ITIL 4's focus on collaboration, feedback, and continual improvement.

Q4: Can you describe a real-world scenario where creative problem-solving was crucial to overcoming an IT challenge?
A4: A notable scenario involved Netflix's transition to cloud services. Faced with the challenge of scaling their infrastructure

to meet growing demand, Netflix employed creative problem-solving to migrate their services to Amazon Web Services (AWS), enabling them to scale rapidly and efficiently. This decision required innovative thinking and a willingness to embrace new technologies, in line with ITIL 4's principles of adaptability and leveraging digital technology.

Q5: Why is it important for IT organizations to foster innovation and creativity?
A5: Fostering innovation and creativity is vital for IT organizations to maintain competitive advantage, adapt to changing technology landscapes, and meet evolving customer needs. It aligns with ITIL 4's emphasis on creating value through services that are continually improved and adapted to the market and user requirements.

Q6: How does ITIL 4's framework facilitate an environment conducive to innovation and creativity within IT organizations?
A6: ITIL 4 facilitates an innovative and creative environment by providing a flexible framework that encourages organizations to adopt and adapt best practices according to their unique circumstances. It promotes a culture of continual improvement, value co-creation, and customer focus, which are essential for nurturing innovation and creativity.

Case Study: Innovatech Solutions Inc.

Background

Innovatech Solutions Inc., a burgeoning software development company, faced significant challenges in maintaining its competitive edge in the rapidly evolving tech industry. Despite having a talented team and a portfolio of successful projects, Innovatech struggled with stagnation in innovation and creativity within its IT department. The leadership recognized the need for a cultural shift towards more innovative practices to foster growth and sustainability.

Challenge

The primary challenge for Innovatech was overcoming the traditional, siloed approach to software development and IT operations that stifled creativity and slowed down the innovation process. The company needed to find a way to encourage creative problem-solving and cultivate an innovative IT organization capable of adapting to technological advancements and customer expectations swiftly.

Solution

Innovatech embarked on a transformation journey guided by ITIL 4 principles to cultivate an environment that nurtures innovation and creativity. The company implemented several strategic changes:

1. **Adopting ITIL 4's Guiding Principles:** Innovatech adopted ITIL 4's guiding principles, particularly focusing on "Start where you are," "Progress iteratively with feedback," and "Collaborate and promote visibility." This encouraged a culture of continuous improvement and open communication.

2. **Creating Cross-functional Teams:** To break down silos, Innovatech reorganized its IT department into cross-functional teams that included members from development, operations, quality assurance, and customer support. This approach facilitated a collaborative environment where diverse perspectives led to innovative solutions.

3. **Encouraging Experimentation:** Innovatech introduced a policy that allowed employees to spend a portion of their time on experimental projects or learning new technologies. Inspired by successful tech companies, this initiative aimed to spur creativity and exploration of novel ideas without the fear of failure.

4. **Implementing Agile and Lean Practices:** By adopting Agile methodologies and Lean practices, Innovatech streamlined its project management processes, which enabled quicker iterations, faster feedback loops, and a focus on delivering value to customers.

5. **Continuous Learning and Development:** Innovatech invested in continuous learning opportunities for its employees, including workshops, online courses, and attendance at industry conferences. This commitment to professional development ensured that the team remained at the forefront of technological advancements.

Results

Within a year of implementing these changes, Innovatech Solutions Inc. observed remarkable improvements in its IT organization's productivity and innovation capacity. The company successfully launched several groundbreaking products that were well-received by the market, leading to increased revenue and market share. Employee satisfaction scores also rose significantly, with many team members expressing a renewed sense of engagement and creativity in their work.

Questions for Discussion

1. How did ITIL 4's guiding principles facilitate a culture of innovation at Innovatech Solutions Inc.?
2. What were the key factors in successfully breaking down silos and fostering collaboration within Innovatech?
3. How can other companies replicate Innovatech's approach to encouraging experimentation and creative problem-solving?
4. What challenges might Innovatech face in maintaining this culture of innovation, and how could they address these challenges using ITIL 4 practices?
5. In what ways did continuous learning contribute to the innovative outcomes achieved by Innovatech? How does this align with ITIL 4's emphasis on continual improvement?

Chapter 15: The Path to Digital Transformation

Introduction

In an era where digital technology is evolving at an unprecedented pace, organizations across various sectors are finding themselves at a crossroads: to digitally transform or to risk obsolescence. Digital transformation is not merely about adopting new technologies; it's a radical rethinking of how an organization uses technology, people, and processes to fundamentally change business performance. This chapter explores the path to digital transformation through the lens of ITIL4, providing a structured approach that integrates robust IT service management with the agility and flexibility required for digital success.

The Essence of Digital Transformation with ITIL4

Digital transformation is a comprehensive process that involves the integration of digital technology into all areas of a business, resulting in fundamental changes to how businesses operate and how they deliver value to customers. More than just a technological upgrade, it is a cultural shift that challenges organizations to continually experiment, adapt, and grow in a fast-paced digital landscape.

ITIL4, with its focus on co-creating business value from IT-supported services, offers a practical framework for navigating digital transformation. It emphasizes the importance of aligning IT services with business needs, adopting agile and lean practices, and fostering a collaborative and customer-focused culture.

Real-Time Examples and Strategies

Several leading companies have exemplified the principles of digital transformation with ITIL4 at their core. For instance, Amazon's relentless focus on customer experience and its use of big data and analytics to drive business decisions reflect ITIL4's principles of focusing on value and keeping the big picture in mind. Amazon's ability to innovate rapidly, experiment, and adapt to market changes underscores the agility that ITIL4 promotes.

Another example is Netflix, which transformed from a DVD rental service to a global streaming giant. Netflix's culture of innovation, its use of cloud computing to scale its operations, and its data-driven approach to content creation are in line with ITIL4's guidance on leveraging technology and information to deliver value.

Strategies for Digital Transformation

Embarking on a digital transformation journey requires a nuanced approach that goes beyond the mere adoption of new technologies. It necessitates a holistic reevaluation of operations, culture, and strategy. Here are detailed strategies for ensuring a successful digital transformation:

1. Align Digital Initiatives with Business Objectives: One of the most critical strategies is ensuring that all digital transformation efforts are in direct alignment with the overarching business goals. This involves a thorough analysis of business objectives and identifying how

digital technologies can enhance or revolutionize the way these objectives are achieved. ITIL4 emphasizes the importance of the Service Value System (SVS) in guiding organizations to ensure that their digital services consistently co-create value. For instance, if a business objective is to improve customer satisfaction, digital initiatives might focus on integrating AI-powered chatbots for 24/7 customer service.

2. Adopt an Agile and Iterative Approach: The dynamic nature of digital technology and customer expectations requires organizations to be flexible and adaptable. Adopting agile methodologies allows for rapid iteration based on user feedback and changing market trends. This approach is supported by ITIL4's continual improvement model, which encourages organizations to undertake smaller, manageable changes that can be evaluated and adjusted in real-time. Agile practices also foster a collaborative environment where cross-functional teams work together towards common goals, enhancing the innovation and speed of digital transformation efforts.

3. Foster a Culture of Continuous Learning and Innovation: Digital transformation is not just about technology; it's equally about the people behind the technology. Cultivating a culture that embraces change, encourages experimentation, and supports continuous learning is vital. ITIL4's guiding principles, such as "Start where you are" and "Progress iteratively with feedback," advocate for this mindset by emphasizing the importance of learning from current operations and gradually implementing changes. This can be seen in organizations like Google, which promotes a culture of innovation through its famous '20% time' policy,

212

allowing employees to spend a portion of their time on side projects, which has led to the creation of products like Gmail and AdSense.

Overcoming Common Pitfalls

While the path to digital transformation holds great promise, it is laden with potential pitfalls. Recognizing and addressing these challenges early is key to a successful digital journey:

1. Resistance to Change: One of the most significant barriers to digital transformation is the natural resistance to change within organizations. This can stem from fear of the unknown, comfort with current processes, or skepticism about the benefits of new technology. Overcoming this resistance requires strong leadership committed to clear, transparent communication about the benefits of digital transformation. Leaders must also actively involve employees in the transformation process, offering training and support to ease the transition and demonstrate the tangible benefits of change.

2. Siloed Operations and Lack of Collaboration: Digital transformation requires a coordinated effort across all departments of an organization. However, siloed operations can impede information sharing and collaboration, leading to disjointed initiatives that fail to leverage the full potential of digital technologies. Breaking down these silos involves fostering a culture of collaboration and ensuring that digital transformation

strategies are integrated and aligned across the organization. ITIL4's emphasis on a holistic approach to service management supports this integration, advocating for cross-functional teams and shared objectives.

3. Overambition and Lack of Focus: Embarking on too many digital initiatives simultaneously can dilute focus and resources, leading to subpar outcomes. Organizations must prioritize their digital efforts, focusing on initiatives that offer the most significant impact and align closely with business goals. This involves careful planning, setting clear metrics for success, and being willing to pivot or adjust strategies based on performance and feedback. ITIL4's service value chain provides a framework for evaluating and prioritizing initiatives based on their potential to create value, ensuring that organizations focus their efforts where they can make the most difference.

In summary, a successful digital transformation strategy requires alignment with business objectives, an agile and iterative approach, and a culture of continuous learning. By recognizing and addressing common pitfalls such as resistance to change, siloed operations, and overambition, organizations can navigate the complexities of digital transformation and emerge stronger, more agile, and better equipped to meet the demands of the digital age.

Conclusion

The journey towards digital transformation is both a challenge and an opportunity for organizations seeking to thrive in the digital age. As we have explored in this chapter, embarking on this path requires a deliberate strategy that aligns digital initiatives with business objectives, leverages agile and iterative methodologies, and fosters a culture of continuous learning and innovation. Through the lens of ITIL4, we've seen how a structured approach to service management can guide organizations in co-creating value with their customers and stakeholders, ensuring that digital transformation efforts lead to sustainable success.

Moreover, understanding and overcoming common pitfalls such as resistance to change, siloed operations, and overambition are crucial to maintaining momentum and achieving the desired outcomes. By fostering strong leadership, encouraging cross-functional collaboration, and prioritizing initiatives based on their value, organizations can navigate these challenges effectively.

Digital transformation is not a destination but a journey of constant evolution and adaptation. In this digital era, the ability to innovate, adapt, and learn continuously is what will differentiate successful organizations from the rest. ITIL4 provides a valuable framework for navigating this journey, offering principles and practices that support organizations in their quest to become more agile, resilient, and customer-focused.

As we conclude this chapter, it's clear that the path to digital transformation is multifaceted, involving much more than just technological change. It requires a holistic rethinking of how organizations operate, how they engage with their customers, and how they define value in a digital context. By embracing the strategies and overcoming the pitfalls discussed, organizations can harness the power of digital technology to not only survive but thrive in the rapidly changing business landscape. The future belongs to those who are prepared to transform, adapt, and lead in the digital age.

Questions and Answers for Chapter 15: The Path to Digital Transformation

1. What is digital transformation, and why is it critical for organizations in the current era?

> **Answer:** Digital transformation involves a comprehensive integration of digital technology into all areas of a business, leading to fundamental changes in how businesses operate and deliver value to customers. It's critical for organizations to stay competitive and relevant in an era where digital technology evolves rapidly, as it enables them to meet changing customer expectations, enhance operational efficiency, and innovate in product and service offerings.

2. How does ITIL4 contribute to the digital transformation journey of an organization?

> **Answer:** ITIL4 provides a structured approach to service management that integrates robust IT service management with the agility and flexibility required for digital success. It emphasizes the importance of aligning IT services with business needs, adopting agile and lean practices, and fostering a collaborative and customer-focused culture, thereby aiding organizations in their digital transformation efforts.

3. Can you give examples of companies that have successfully implemented digital transformation principles aligned with ITIL4?

> **Answer:** Amazon and Netflix are prime examples. Amazon has focused relentlessly on customer experience and utilized big data and analytics to drive business decisions, reflecting ITIL4's principles. Similarly, Netflix's transformation from a

DVD rental service to a streaming giant, leveraging cloud computing and a data-driven content strategy, aligns with ITIL4's guidance on leveraging technology and information to deliver value.

4. What are the key strategies for achieving a successful digital transformation?

Answer: The key strategies include aligning digital initiatives with business objectives, adopting an agile and iterative approach, and fostering a culture of continuous learning and innovation. These strategies ensure that digital transformation efforts are directly tied to enhancing business performance and are executed in a flexible, responsive manner that encourages innovation.

5. How can organizations overcome the common pitfalls encountered during digital transformation?

Answer: Organizations can overcome common pitfalls by ensuring strong leadership and clear communication to overcome resistance to change, fostering a culture of collaboration to break down silos, and prioritizing digital efforts to avoid overambition and lack of focus. These steps help maintain momentum and achieve successful outcomes in digital transformation projects.

6. Why is it important to prioritize digital initiatives based on their potential impact on business objectives and customer value?

Answer: Prioritizing digital initiatives based on their impact ensures that resources are focused on projects that offer the most significant benefits to the business and its customers. This strategic approach helps organizations avoid spreading their efforts too thinly across too many projects, enabling them to achieve tangible results that contribute to business growth and customer satisfaction.

7. In what ways does digital transformation go beyond technological change?

Answer: Digital transformation goes beyond technological change by also encompassing a cultural shift within organizations. It requires a holistic rethinking of operations, how organizations engage with their customers, and how they define value in a digital context. This multifaceted approach involves changing mindsets, processes, and business models to fully leverage the opportunities presented by digital technologies.

8. What role does continuous learning and innovation play in digital transformation?

Answer: Continuous learning and innovation are vital to digital transformation as they enable organizations to adapt to the rapid pace of technological change, experiment with new ideas, and remain competitive. Cultivating a culture that embraces change and encourages innovation ensures that organizations can continuously improve and innovate their products, services, and processes in response to evolving market demands and technological advancements.

Case Study: Digital Transformation at Global Tech Solutions

Background:

Global Tech Solutions, a mid-sized software company specializing in cloud services, recognized the need to undergo a digital transformation to stay competitive in the rapidly evolving tech industry. Despite having a robust IT infrastructure, the company was struggling to meet changing customer expectations and enhance its product offerings due to outdated processes and a lack of strategic alignment between its IT initiatives and business goals.

Challenge:

The primary challenge for Global Tech Solutions was to realign its IT strategy with the company's broader business objectives to drive growth and innovation. The company faced several issues, including resistance to change among staff, siloed departments leading to a lack of collaboration and innovation, and an overabundance of ongoing IT projects with unclear business value.

Strategy:

1. Strategic Alignment: The company's leadership team, with the help of IT governance experts, revisited the organization's strategic objectives and redefined the IT strategy to support these goals. They focused on digital initiatives that could drive customer satisfaction and operational efficiency.

2. Adopting an Agile Approach: Global Tech Solutions adopted agile methodologies across its teams to improve flexibility and responsiveness to customer feedback and market changes. This approach encouraged iterative development, continuous delivery, and a focus on customer value.

3. Fostering a Culture of Continuous Learning and Innovation: The company launched a series of workshops and training programs aimed at promoting a culture of innovation and continuous improvement

among employees. They also introduced a digital innovation lab where teams could work on experimental projects.

4. Overcoming Common Pitfalls:

    - Leadership and Communication: To overcome resistance to change, the leadership team led by example, clearly communicated the vision and benefits of digital transformation, and actively involved employees in the change process.

    - Breaking Down Silos: The company restructured its teams to encourage cross-functional collaboration and integrated digital strategies across the organization.

    - Prioritizing Initiatives: They established a clear framework for evaluating and prioritizing IT projects based on their potential impact on business objectives and customer value.

Outcome:

Within 18 months, Global Tech Solutions saw significant improvements in operational efficiency, customer satisfaction, and market competitiveness. Their agile transformation led to faster product development cycles and the ability to quickly adapt to customer needs. The focus on strategic alignment and prioritization of digital initiatives resulted in a clearer direction and more effective use of resources. Additionally, the culture of innovation and continuous learning led to the development of new, cutting-edge products and services.

Questions and Answers:

1. Q: How did Global Tech Solutions address the challenge of strategic misalignment between IT and business goals?

2. Q: What methodologies did Global Tech Solutions adopt to improve flexibility and responsiveness?

3. Q: How did Global Tech Solutions foster a culture of innovation and continuous improvement?

4. Q: What steps did Global Tech Solutions take to overcome resistance to change and ensure the success of its digital transformation?

5. Q: How did prioritizing IT projects based on their potential impact on business objectives and customer value benefit Global Tech Solutions?

Chapter 16: Emerging Trends and Future Technologies

Introduction

As we stand on the brink of a technological revolution that will fundamentally alter the way we live, work, and relate to one another, the scale, scope, and complexity of the impact of emerging technologies will be unlike anything humanity has experienced before. This chapter delves into the forefront of this transformation, exploring emerging trends such as quantum computing, edge computing, and beyond. Drawing upon frameworks like ITIL and COBIT, we illuminate how organizations can navigate these changes, harnessing the power of innovation while ensuring strategic alignment, operational excellence, and robust governance. Through real-life examples, we will explore the practical applications of these technologies and the strategies that leading companies are employing to future-proof their operations in this ever-evolving landscape.

Quantum Computing: The Next Frontier

Quantum computing promises to mark a paradigm shift in our computational capabilities, leveraging the principles of quantum mechanics to process information in ways that traditional computers cannot match. This technology is poised to revolutionize fields such as cryptography, drug discovery, and artificial intelligence, offering new horizons of efficiency and problem-solving capabilities.

Real-Life Example: Google's quantum supremacy experiment with its 54-qubit processor, Sycamore, demonstrated the potential of quantum computing to perform specific tasks exponentially faster than the most powerful classical supercomputers available today.

Strategic Alignment with ITIL and COBIT: The implementation of quantum computing technologies presents unique challenges and opportunities for IT governance and service management. ITIL's focus on aligning IT services with business needs ensures that investments in quantum computing are driven by clear strategic objectives, while COBIT's governance framework provides the structure needed to manage the risks and maximize the benefits of these advanced technologies.

Edge Computing: Processing at the Edge

Edge computing represents a shift towards processing data closer to the source of data generation, enhancing the speed and efficiency of data handling. This approach is critical for real-time applications requiring rapid processing, such as IoT devices, autonomous vehicles, and smart city technologies.

Real-Life Example: Amazon Web Services (AWS) Wavelength brings AWS compute and storage services to the edge of telecommunications networks, reducing latency for mobile and connected devices, and enabling developers to build ultra-low latency applications.

Leveraging ITIL and COBIT: Adopting edge computing requires a reevaluation of IT service management and governance practices. ITIL provides a framework for managing IT services that can adapt to the decentralized nature of edge computing, focusing on delivering value and managing risks. COBIT, with its emphasis on governance and management of enterprise IT, offers a comprehensive approach to overseeing the deployment and operation of edge computing infrastructure, ensuring alignment with business goals and compliance with regulatory requirements.

Preparing for the Unknown: Future-Proof Strategies

The pace of technological advancement necessitates that organizations not only adapt to current trends but also prepare for future disruptions. Future-proofing strategies involve fostering a culture of innovation, agility, and continuous learning.

Real-Life Example: SpaceX's development of reusable rockets demonstrates the power of visionary thinking and continuous innovation. By challenging the traditional norms of space travel, SpaceX has reduced the cost of space exploration and opened new possibilities for the future.

Adapting with ITIL and COBIT: Future-proofing in the context of ITIL involves embracing the principle of continual improvement, ensuring that IT services remain aligned with evolving business needs and technological capabilities. COBIT's framework supports this by providing a structured approach to governance and management, emphasizing flexibility, strategic planning, and risk management.

Quantum Computing, Edge Computing, and Beyond

The digital frontier is expanding into realms once considered the domain of science fiction, with quantum computing and edge computing leading the charge. Quantum computing transcends traditional binary computing by harnessing quantum bits (qubits) to perform complex calculations at unprecedented speeds. This leap forward offers transformative potential for fields ranging from cryptography, where it could render current encryption methods obsolete, to pharmaceuticals, by drastically accelerating drug discovery processes. A notable milestone was achieved by IBM, which unveiled its quantum computer capable of handling 53 qubits, signaling a significant advancement towards practical quantum computing applications.

Edge computing, in contrast, decentralizes data processing, pushing it closer to the source of data generation. This shift is crucial for applications requiring real-time processing, such as autonomous vehicle navigation systems, which cannot tolerate the latency introduced by distant data centers. For instance, Volvo Cars has partnered with Ericsson to utilize edge computing in enhancing vehicle connectivity and autonomous driving capabilities, demonstrating how edge computing enables real-time data processing critical for safety and efficiency on the roads.

These technologies, while at different stages of maturity, signify a move towards a more interconnected, efficient, and high-speed digital world. Their evolution will undoubtedly bring forth new challenges and opportunities, underscoring the importance of adaptive and forward-thinking IT governance and service management strategies.

Preparing for the Unknown: Future-Proof Strategies

In a technological landscape characterized by rapid and unpredictable change, organizations must adopt future-proof strategies that enable them to adapt and thrive. This necessitates a culture of continuous innovation, agility, and learning, underpinned by robust governance frameworks like ITIL and COBIT.

Google's approach to innovation, with its famed policy of allowing employees to dedicate 20% of their time to side projects, exemplifies a culture that encourages experimentation and creativity. This policy has led to the development of key services like Gmail and AdSense, illustrating how fostering an environment that values innovation can yield substantial dividends.

Similarly, Netflix's pivot from DVD rentals to streaming services demonstrates strategic agility. By recognizing and acting on the shift in consumer preferences towards digital content, Netflix not only survived the transition but thrived, becoming a dominant force in the entertainment industry. This adaptability was facilitated by a clear vision and the willingness to embrace change, even when it meant disrupting its existing business model.

To prepare for the unknown, organizations should leverage ITIL's continual improvement model and COBIT's governance and management frameworks to establish flexible strategies that can accommodate evolving technologies and market demands. This includes investing in ongoing education and training for staff, fostering a culture of innovation and flexibility, and implementing robust risk management practices to mitigate potential disruptions. By doing so, organizations can navigate the uncertainties of the digital age, seizing opportunities and mitigating risks as they arise.

Conclusion

As we conclude our exploration into the realms of quantum computing, edge computing, and the necessity of preparing for the unknown through future-proof strategies, it's evident that the technological landscape is undergoing a transformation that is both profound and unprecedented. The advancements in quantum and edge computing not only promise to elevate computational capabilities and efficiency but also challenge existing paradigms of data processing and application development. The journey of companies like IBM in quantum computing and Volvo Cars in leveraging edge computing for autonomous driving highlights the tangible strides being made towards harnessing these technologies for real-world applications.

Moreover, the stories of Google's innovative culture and Netflix's strategic agility underscore the critical importance of embracing change and fostering an environment that prioritizes continuous learning, flexibility, and innovation. These examples serve as powerful reminders that the future belongs to those who are prepared to question the status quo, experiment boldly, and pivot swiftly in response to new challenges and opportunities.

In navigating this rapidly evolving technological frontier, frameworks such as ITIL and COBIT offer valuable guidance, ensuring that organizations can align their IT strategies with business objectives, manage risks effectively, and cultivate a governance culture that supports sustainable growth and innovation. By embedding principles of continual improvement, strategic flexibility, and robust governance into their core operations, organizations can not only mitigate the risks associated with emerging technologies but also position themselves to capitalize on the opportunities they present.

Ultimately, the journey towards mastering quantum computing, edge computing, and other emerging technologies, while navigating the uncertainties of the digital age, is a complex but rewarding endeavor. It requires a commitment to strategic foresight, operational excellence, and a culture that values adaptability and innovation. As we look to the future, it is clear that those organizations that embrace these principles, leveraging the insights and frameworks provided by ITIL and

COBIT, will be best positioned to thrive in an era of rapid technological change and to make significant contributions to shaping the future of our digital world.

Questions and Answers for Chapter 16: Emerging Trends and Future Technologies

1. What are the key characteristics that differentiate quantum computing from traditional computing?

- **Answer:** Quantum computing differs from traditional computing in its use of quantum bits or qubits, which can represent and process information in a way that allows for much more complex computations at significantly faster speeds. Unlike traditional binary bits, which can be either 0 or 1, qubits can exist in multiple states simultaneously thanks to the principles of superposition and entanglement, enabling quantum computers to perform many calculations in parallel.

2. How does edge computing enhance the capabilities of real-time data processing applications?

- **Answer:** Edge computing enhances real-time data processing by bringing computation and data storage closer to the location where it is needed, minimizing latency. This is crucial for applications such as autonomous vehicles, IoT devices, and smart city technologies, where processing speed and immediate response times are essential for functionality and safety.

3. Can you give an example of a company that has successfully integrated edge computing into its operations?

- **Answer:** Volvo Cars has successfully integrated edge computing into its operations, particularly in enhancing vehicle connectivity and autonomous driving capabilities. By partnering with Ericsson to use edge computing, Volvo has been able to process real-time data more efficiently, improving safety and driving experiences.

4. What is the significance of Google's "20% time" policy in fostering an innovative culture?

- **Answer:** Google's "20% time" policy is significant because it encourages employees to dedicate a portion of their working hours to exploring new ideas and side projects that interest them. This policy fosters a culture of creativity and innovation, leading to the development of successful products like Gmail and AdSense, and underscores the value of allowing space for experimentation and risk-taking in driving technological advancements.

5. How did Netflix's strategic pivot contribute to its success in the digital age?

- **Answer:** Netflix's strategic pivot from DVD rentals to streaming services contributed to its success by demonstrating the company's agility and willingness to embrace change. Recognizing the shift in consumer preferences towards digital content, Netflix adapted its business model to focus on streaming, leveraging new technologies to deliver a vast library of content directly to consumers. This not only helped Netflix survive the transition but also thrive as a leader in the entertainment industry.

6. Why are frameworks like ITIL and COBIT important for organizations navigating emerging technologies?

- **Answer:** Frameworks like ITIL and COBIT are important because they provide structured guidance on aligning IT services and governance with business objectives, managing risks, and ensuring operational excellence. As organizations navigate the complexities of emerging technologies, these frameworks help ensure that technological innovations are implemented in a way that supports strategic goals, enhances efficiency, and maintains robust governance and risk management practices.

7. What strategies can organizations employ to future-proof their operations against the uncertainties of technological advancements?

- **Answer:** To future-proof their operations, organizations can foster a culture of continuous learning and innovation, embrace strategic flexibility, invest in workforce development, and implement robust risk management practices. Emphasizing continuous improvement and adaptability ensures that organizations can respond effectively to technological changes and capitalize on new opportunities.

8. How can scenario planning aid organizations in preparing for future technological trends?

- **Answer:** Scenario planning aids organizations by allowing them to develop and analyze a range of possible futures based on different technological trends and market developments. This process helps organizations anticipate potential impacts, prepare strategic responses, and remain agile in the face of uncertainty. By considering various scenarios, organizations can better position themselves to navigate the challenges and seize the opportunities presented by emerging technologies.

Case Study: NextGen Technologies, Inc.

Background:

NextGen Technologies, Inc., a leading technology firm based in Silicon Valley, has been at the forefront of adopting emerging technologies to maintain its market leadership. Recognizing the transformative potential of quantum computing and edge computing, NextGen embarked on a journey to integrate these technologies into their product offerings. Furthermore, the company sought to future-proof its strategies to adapt swiftly to technological advancements and market shifts.

Quantum Computing Initiative:

NextGen Technologies invested heavily in quantum computing research, aiming to develop a quantum computing platform that could revolutionize data encryption and security. This platform was designed to offer unprecedented computational power to solve complex problems, which were previously considered infeasible for classical computers.

Edge Computing Deployment:

To enhance its IoT solutions, NextGen also embraced edge computing, deploying edge servers closer to IoT devices to process data in real-time. This initiative aimed to reduce latency, improve efficiency, and support advanced applications such as autonomous vehicles and smart city infrastructures.

Challenges Faced:

1. **Technical Complexity:** The development and integration of quantum and edge computing technologies posed significant technical challenges, requiring specialized knowledge and skills.

2. **Cultural Resistance:** NextGen faced resistance from within, as employees were accustomed to traditional computing paradigms and wary of the uncertainties associated with these new technologies.

3. **Strategic Alignment:** Ensuring that these initiatives aligned with the company's broader strategic objectives required a reevaluation of NextGen's IT governance and service management practices.

Strategies for Success:

To address these challenges, NextGen adopted several key strategies:

1. **Leveraging ITIL and COBIT:** NextGen utilized ITIL principles to align its IT services with business needs and employed COBIT to manage risks and ensure robust governance of its new technological ventures.

2. **Fostering a Culture of Innovation:** The company initiated programs to encourage continuous learning and innovation, including workshops, hackathons, and partnerships with academic institutions.

3. **Strategic Flexibility:** NextGen adopted an agile approach to project management, allowing for rapid

iteration and adaptation based on feedback and emerging trends.

Outcomes:

NextGen Technologies successfully integrated quantum and edge computing into its product lines, leading to significant improvements in data security and processing efficiency. The company not only enhanced its competitive edge but also positioned itself as a leader in driving technological innovation.

Case Study Questions:

1. How did NextGen Technologies address the technical complexity associated with quantum and edge computing?

2. What strategies did NextGen employ to overcome cultural resistance to new technologies within the organization?

3. How did leveraging ITIL and COBIT frameworks contribute to the successful integration of emerging technologies at NextGen?

4. In what ways did NextGen foster a culture of innovation to support its technological initiatives?

5. Discuss the importance of strategic flexibility in NextGen's approach to adopting quantum and edge computing. How did this flexibility impact the project outcomes?

6. Reflecting on NextGen's experience, what lessons can be learned about future-proofing an organization's strategies in the face of rapid technological advancements?

Chapter 17: Building a Learning Organization

Introduction

The transformation into a learning organization is a strategic journey that enables businesses to thrive in the face of change and uncertainty. This evolution fosters an environment where continuous learning, adaptability, and innovation are part of the organizational DNA. In such organizations, learning transcends individual employees, becoming a collective goal that propels the entire organization forward. This chapter explores the concept of learning organizations, underscored with real-life examples, and delves into the myriad ways staff and stakeholders benefit from this culture. It also highlights the crucial roles of training initiatives and management support in cultivating such an environment.

Real-Life Examples

Siemens AG: Siemens, a global powerhouse in electronics and electrical engineering, exemplifies a learning organization. Through its comprehensive learning and development programs, Siemens invests in the continuous growth of its employees, focusing on leadership, technical skills, and innovation. Its proactive approach to learning has enabled Siemens to remain at the forefront of technological advancements and maintain a competitive edge in its industry.

Pixar Animation Studios: Another illustrative example is Pixar Animation Studios, renowned for its creative prowess and cutting-edge animation. Pixar fosters a collaborative and open learning environment where mistakes are viewed as opportunities for growth. Regular "postmortem" meetings after project completions ensure lessons are learned and shared, driving continuous improvement and innovation.

Benefits to Staff and Other Stakeholders

The transition into a learning organization yields significant benefits for both staff and stakeholders:

For Staff:

- Skill Enhancement: Continuous learning opportunities allow employees to enhance their skills and competencies, keeping them relevant in a rapidly changing job market.

- Career Growth: Learning organizations often have clear pathways for career advancement, as they prioritize internal talent development for leadership and specialized roles.

- Increased Engagement: A culture that values learning and development contributes to higher employee engagement, satisfaction, and retention.

For Stakeholders:

- Innovation and Competitiveness: Stakeholders benefit from the organization's capacity for innovation and adaptation, which drives long-term competitiveness and market leadership.

- Organizational Agility: Learning organizations are better equipped to respond to changes in the market or industry, safeguarding stakeholders' interests.

- Enhanced Reputation: Being recognized as a learning organization can enhance the brand's reputation, attracting talent and investment.

Involvement of Trainings and Management Support

Training Initiatives:

Training initiatives are pivotal in building a learning organization. These include:

- Customized Learning Plans: Tailoring learning and development plans to individual needs and career aspirations.

- Leveraging Technology: Utilizing e-learning platforms and digital tools to make learning accessible and flexible.

- Creating Learning Spaces: Establishing physical and virtual spaces that encourage collaboration, creativity, and sharing of knowledge.

Management Support:

The role of management is critical in fostering a learning culture:

- Vision and Commitment: Leadership must articulate a clear vision for the learning organization and demonstrate commitment through resources and policies.

- Encouraging Participation: Managers should encourage and facilitate participation in learning activities, recognizing and rewarding engagement.

- Modeling Behaviors: Leaders must model the desired behaviors, showing their own commitment to continuous learning and development.

Importance of Continuous Learning in IT

The realm of Information Technology (IT) is a landscape of unceasing evolution, where the only constant is change itself. In such an environment, the importance of continuous learning cannot be overstated. It serves as the backbone of innovation and adaptability, enabling individuals and organizations alike to stay competitive in the global marketplace.

Continuous learning in IT is crucial for several reasons:

- **Adaptability:** With technological advancements happening at a breakneck pace, the ability to adapt to new technologies, processes, and methodologies is vital. Continuous learning ensures that IT professionals and organizations are not left behind as the industry evolves.

- **Innovation:** Learning new skills and technologies fosters innovation. It allows individuals and organizations to explore new possibilities, develop novel solutions, and lead the way in technological advancements.

- **Professional Growth:** For IT professionals, continuous learning is key to career advancement. It enables them to keep their skills relevant and opens up opportunities for higher responsibilities and roles.

- **Organizational Competitiveness:** From an organizational perspective, a workforce committed to continuous learning is more agile, innovative, and better equipped to respond to market demands. This drives growth and ensures long-term success.

Resources and Approaches for Staying Ahead

To embrace continuous learning, both individuals and organizations in the IT sector must utilize a variety of resources and approaches. Here are some effective strategies:

Formal Education and Certifications

Enrolling in formal education programs, such as degree courses or specialized IT certifications, can provide a structured learning path and validate one's skills in specific technologies or methodologies. Certifications from recognized bodies or vendors are particularly valuable in the IT industry.

Online Learning Platforms

Platforms like Coursera, Udemy, and LinkedIn Learning offer a vast array of courses covering various IT disciplines. These platforms are ideal for learning at one's own pace and are often updated with the latest content in technology trends.

Workshops, Seminars, and Conferences

Participating in workshops, seminars, and conferences provides opportunities to learn from leading experts and practitioners in the field. It also offers a platform for networking with peers, sharing knowledge, and staying informed about the latest industry developments.

Internal Training Programs

Organizations can develop internal training programs tailored to their specific needs and technologies. This could include mentorship programs, lunch-and-learn sessions, and internal courses. Such programs not only upskill the workforce but also foster a culture of learning and knowledge sharing.

Peer Learning and Collaboration

Encouraging collaboration and knowledge sharing among employees can be a powerful way to facilitate continuous learning. Tools like internal wikis, forums, and regular tech meet-ups can help create a collaborative environment that promotes learning.

Support from Management

Management support is crucial in building a culture of continuous learning. This includes providing resources for learning, recognizing and rewarding learning achievements, and integrating learning into the organizational strategy.

By leveraging these resources and approaches, IT professionals and organizations can ensure they are always at the forefront of technological advancements, ready to meet the challenges and opportunities of the digital age. Continuous learning in IT is not just about staying relevant; it's about driving progress, fostering innovation, and achieving excellence.

Conclusion

In conclusion, the imperative for continuous learning in the IT sector is both undeniable and critical for individual and organizational success in an era of relentless technological advancement. This chapter has underscored the importance of embracing a culture of perpetual growth and adaptability, highlighting how such a mindset is essential not only for staying relevant but also for driving innovation and maintaining a competitive edge.

Through real-life examples and a detailed exploration of various resources and approaches, we've seen that continuous learning can take many forms, from formal education and certifications to online platforms and internal training programs. Each avenue offers unique benefits and, when combined, can create a comprehensive learning ecosystem that supports the diverse needs of IT professionals and organizations.

The involvement of all stakeholders, particularly the support from management, is paramount in fostering an environment where learning is valued, encouraged, and integrated into the very fabric of the organizational culture. This support transforms learning from an individual pursuit into a collective endeavor that benefits everyone involved, leading to enhanced innovation, improved job satisfaction, and ultimately, sustained organizational success.

As we move forward, the principles and strategies discussed in this chapter serve as a roadmap for building and nurturing a learning organization. The journey towards becoming a learning organization is ongoing, requiring commitment, investment, and a strategic approach to continuous improvement. However, the rewards—ranging from personal growth and professional development to organizational resilience and innovation—make this journey not just worthwhile but essential.

In essence, the cultivation of a learning organization in the IT sector is not just about keeping pace with technological change; it's about embracing and leading that change. By committing to continuous learning, individuals and organizations can unlock their full potential, ensuring not only their survival in a competitive landscape but their ability to thrive and shape the future of technology.

Questions and Answers Based on the Chapter

Q1: Why is continuous learning particularly important in the IT sector?
A1: Continuous learning is crucial in the IT sector due to the rapid pace of technological advancements. It ensures individuals and organizations remain adaptable, innovative, and competitive by staying up-to-date with the latest technologies, methodologies, and industry best practices.

Q2: What are some effective strategies for individuals and organizations to stay ahead in the IT industry?
A2: Effective strategies include engaging in formal education and obtaining certifications, leveraging online learning platforms, participating in workshops, seminars, and conferences, developing internal training programs, fostering a culture of peer learning and collaboration, and ensuring management support for learning initiatives.

Q3: How can online learning platforms benefit IT professionals?
A3: Online learning platforms provide IT professionals with flexible, self-paced learning options that cover a wide range of topics. These platforms are often updated with the latest content, making it easier for professionals to acquire new skills and stay abreast of current trends and technologies.

Q4: What role does management play in fostering a learning organization within the IT sector?
A4: Management plays a crucial role by providing resources, recognizing and rewarding learning achievements, integrating learning into organizational strategy, and creating an environment that values and encourages continuous improvement and knowledge sharing.

Q5: Can you give an example of how internal training programs can benefit an IT organization?
A5: Internal training programs, tailored to an organization's specific needs and technologies, help upskill employees in areas that are directly relevant to their work. These programs can include mentorship, lunch-and-learn sessions, and in-house courses, fostering a culture of learning and collaboration that benefits both individual growth and organizational success.

Q6: Why is peer learning and collaboration important in building a learning organization?
A6: Peer learning and collaboration encourage knowledge sharing among employees, leveraging the diverse skills and experiences within the organization. This not only enhances individual learning but also fosters innovation and problem-solving, contributing to a dynamic and adaptable organizational culture.

Q7: How do formal education and certifications contribute to continuous learning in IT?
A7: Formal education and certifications provide structured learning paths and validate the expertise of IT professionals in specific technologies or methodologies. They are especially valuable in the IT industry for career advancement, professional credibility, and ensuring that skills are current and relevant.

Q8: What are the long-term benefits of building a learning organization in the IT sector?

A8: Long-term benefits include sustained innovation, improved competitiveness, enhanced employee satisfaction and retention, and the ability to adapt quickly to market changes and technological advancements. Ultimately, a learning organization is better positioned to achieve excellence and lead in the digital age.

Case Study: Transforming TechCo into a Learning Organization

TechCo, a mid-sized software development company, found itself struggling to keep pace with rapid technological changes in the industry. Despite having a talented workforce, the company noticed a growing gap in skills and knowledge, affecting its ability to innovate and meet market demands. Recognizing the need for change, TechCo embarked on a journey to transform itself into a learning organization.

Initiative 1: Implementing a Comprehensive Learning and Development Program
TechCo introduced a comprehensive learning and development program that included access to online courses, certification opportunities, and in-house training workshops. The program was designed to cover a wide range of topics, from emerging technologies to soft skills enhancement.

Initiative 2: Fostering a Culture of Knowledge Sharing
To encourage knowledge sharing and collaboration, TechCo established regular tech talk sessions where employees could present on recent projects, share new technologies, or discuss challenges. Additionally, the company launched an internal knowledge-sharing platform, enabling employees to easily share resources, tutorials, and best practices.

Initiative 3: Encouraging Innovation through Hackathons
TechCo organized quarterly hackathons, providing a fun and

competitive environment for employees to experiment with new ideas and technologies. These events not only fostered innovation but also enhanced team collaboration and problem-solving skills.

Initiative 4: Management Support and Recognition
Management played a crucial role in the transformation by actively supporting learning initiatives. This included allocating budget for professional development, recognizing and rewarding employees' learning achievements, and incorporating learning goals into the company's strategic planning.

Outcome
Within a year, TechCo noticed significant improvements. The workforce became more adaptable and proficient with new technologies, innovation flourished, and employee satisfaction levels rose. The company regained its competitive edge, evidenced by an increase in successful project deliveries and new client acquisitions.

Case Study Questions

Q1: How did TechCo identify the need to become a learning organization?
Q2: What strategies did TechCo implement to encourage continuous learning among its employees?
Q3: How did the introduction of tech talk sessions and hackathons contribute to building a culture of learning and innovation at TechCo?
Q4: What role did management play in transforming TechCo into a learning organization?
Q5: Evaluate the outcomes of TechCo's initiatives to become a learning organization. Which metrics would you use to measure success?
Q6: If you were to propose an additional initiative to further enhance learning at TechCo, what would it be and why?

Q7: Discuss the potential challenges TechCo might face in maintaining its learning organization status and how it could address them.

Chapter 18: The CIO's Roadmap for the Future

Introduction

As the digital landscape continues to evolve at an unprecedented rate, the role of the Chief Information Officer (CIO) has expanded beyond managing IT operations to becoming a strategic partner in shaping the future of business. Today's CIOs are pivotal in driving digital transformation, fostering innovation, and navigating the complexities of emerging technologies. This chapter explores the roadmap for

CIOs as they lead their organizations into the future, emphasizing strategic planning, adaptability, and the alignment of IT initiatives with broader business goals.

The Evolving Role of the CIO

The role of the CIO has transformed significantly over the years, from overseeing back-office IT functions to playing a central role in strategic decision-making. CIOs are now expected to be visionaries, innovators, and change agents who can leverage technology to create competitive advantages, improve customer experiences, and drive organizational growth.

Real-Life Examples from the IT Perspective

Example 1: Transforming Healthcare with Digital Innovation

At a leading healthcare provider, the CIO spearheaded the implementation of a digital health platform that integrated wearable technology, telehealth services, and AI-powered diagnostics. This initiative not only enhanced patient care but also increased operational efficiency and opened new revenue streams. By focusing on digital innovation, the CIO was instrumental in transforming healthcare delivery and positioning the organization as a leader in the industry.

Example 2: Leveraging Data Analytics for Retail Success

In the competitive retail sector, a forward-thinking CIO utilized advanced data analytics to reshape the company's marketing strategies. By analyzing customer data, the organization was able to personalize marketing efforts, optimize inventory management, and improve customer satisfaction. This strategic use of data analytics under the CIO's leadership significantly increased sales and customer loyalty.

Example 3: Driving Financial Services Transformation

A financial services firm's CIO led the development of a blockchain-based transaction system, enhancing security, transparency, and efficiency. This initiative not only streamlined operations but also provided a robust framework for future innovations in fintech. The CIO's focus on cutting-edge technology and its strategic application propelled the firm to the forefront of financial innovation.

Navigating the Future: Key Considerations for CIOs

To effectively guide their organizations into the future, CIOs must focus on several key areas:

- Strategic Alignment: Ensuring that IT initiatives are closely aligned with the organization's strategic objectives and business goals.

- Innovation and Agility: Fostering a culture of innovation and maintaining agility to adapt to rapidly changing technologies and market conditions.

- Cybersecurity and Risk Management: Prioritizing cybersecurity and developing comprehensive risk management strategies to protect organizational assets.

- Talent Management: Attracting, developing, and retaining IT talent to build a skilled, agile, and innovative IT workforce.

- Stakeholder Engagement: Collaborating with stakeholders across the organization to drive digital transformation efforts and ensure the strategic value of IT investments.

Actionable Strategies for Future-Proofing Your IT Organization

Future-proofing an IT organization involves preparing it to handle upcoming challenges and opportunities while maintaining its relevance and efficiency in the face of technological advancements. For CIOs, this means adopting a proactive and strategic approach to technology management and organizational development. Here are some actionable strategies:

- Embrace Agile and DevOps Practices: Implement agile methodologies and DevOps practices to enhance collaboration, speed up software development cycles, and improve the quality of IT services. This approach encourages adaptability and rapid response to changes, which is crucial for future-proofing.

- Invest in Emerging Technologies: Stay abreast of emerging technologies such as artificial intelligence (AI), blockchain, Internet of Things (IoT), and cloud computing. Evaluate their potential impact on your business and invest in those that align with your strategic goals. Pilot projects can help assess their viability and integration into existing systems.

- Foster a Culture of Continuous Learning: Encourage continuous learning and skill development among your IT staff. Provide access to training programs, workshops, and seminars. Emphasizing upskilling and reskilling ensures your team remains adept at leveraging new technologies and methodologies.

- Enhance Cybersecurity Measures: As technology evolves, so do cyber threats. Strengthen your cybersecurity framework by implementing advanced security technologies, conducting regular risk assessments, and promoting cybersecurity awareness throughout the organization.

- Leverage Data Analytics: Utilize data analytics to gain insights into operational efficiency, customer behavior, and market trends. These insights can inform strategic decisions, enhance customer experiences, and identify new opportunities for innovation.

- Adopt a Customer-Centric Approach: Align IT initiatives with customer needs and expectations. This involves developing a deep understanding of your customers and using technology to enhance their experience, thereby ensuring your IT organization remains relevant and valuable.

Creating a Sustainable Competitive Advantage

Creating a sustainable competitive advantage involves leveraging IT not just for operational efficiency but as a strategic asset that differentiates your organization from competitors. Here are strategies to achieve this:

- Strategic IT Alignment: Ensure that IT strategies are fully aligned with business strategies and objectives. This alignment empowers your organization to leverage technology for achieving business goals, such as entering new markets, enhancing product offerings, and improving customer service.

- Innovate Business Models: Use technology to innovate business models. For example, adopting a Software as a Service (SaaS) model can open new revenue streams and increase the scalability of your offerings. Innovation can also involve using technology to create new value propositions that set you apart from competitors.

- Build Digital Ecosystems: Develop partnerships and collaborations that extend your IT capabilities and offerings. By participating in or creating digital ecosystems, you can offer more comprehensive solutions to your customers, leveraging the strengths and innovations of partners.

- Prioritize User Experience (UX): Invest in technologies and design principles that enhance the user experience of your products and services. A superior UX can be a significant differentiator in the market, leading to higher customer satisfaction and loyalty.

- Implement Strategic IT Governance: Develop a governance model that supports decision-making processes, prioritizes IT investments based on strategic value, and manages risks effectively. Strategic IT governance ensures that your IT organization is agile, responsive, and aligned with business goals.

By focusing on these strategies, CIOs can future-proof their IT organizations and create a sustainable competitive advantage. This involves not only adopting the latest technologies but also aligning IT initiatives with business strategies, fostering innovation, and emphasizing customer-centric approaches. Through these efforts, IT organizations can become key drivers of growth, innovation, and long-term success in the digital age.

Conclusion

In conclusion, the roadmap for the future presented to CIOs is both challenging and exciting, laden with opportunities to drive significant change and value within their organizations. As the digital landscape evolves, so too must the strategies and approaches of IT leadership. This chapter has laid out a comprehensive guide for CIOs to not only navigate the complexities of the digital age but also to leverage these challenges as opportunities for growth and innovation.

Future-proofing the IT organization requires a proactive and forward-thinking approach, emphasizing the importance of agility, continuous learning, and investment in emerging technologies. By embracing these actionable strategies, CIOs can ensure that their IT departments are not just prepared for the future but are actively shaping it.

Creating a sustainable competitive advantage goes beyond mere technological adoption; it involves rethinking business models, cultivating digital ecosystems, and placing a premium on customer experience. These efforts necessitate a strategic alignment of IT initiatives with broader business objectives, ensuring that technology serves as a catalyst for growth and differentiation.

The role of the CIO in this journey is pivotal. As strategic partners, innovators, and change agents, CIOs hold the key to unlocking the potential of their organizations in the digital era. The success of their mission hinges on their ability to foster a culture of innovation, manage cybersecurity risks, and build a skilled and adaptable IT workforce.

As we look to the future, it is clear that the landscape of IT and digital business will continue to evolve at an accelerated pace. The strategies outlined in this chapter provide a roadmap for CIOs to not only keep pace with this evolution but to lead their organizations to new heights of success and innovation. The journey ahead is fraught with challenges, but for the CIOs who navigate it wisely, the opportunities are boundless.

Questions and Answers for Chapter 18: The CIO's Roadmap for the Future

Q1: What role do Agile and DevOps practices play in future-proofing an IT organization?
A1: Agile and DevOps practices are crucial for future-proofing an IT organization as they enhance collaboration, speed up development cycles, improve service quality, and ensure the organization can adapt quickly to changes in technology and business environments.

Q2: Why is investing in emerging technologies important for IT organizations?
A2: Investing in emerging technologies is important because it allows IT organizations to stay ahead of technological advancements, explore new business opportunities, and maintain a competitive edge by leveraging technologies that align with their strategic goals.

Q3: How can continuous learning and skill development contribute to the future-proofing of an IT team?
A3: Continuous learning and skill development ensure that the IT team remains proficient in new technologies and methodologies, which is vital for adapting to changes, solving complex problems, and driving innovation within the organization.

Q4: In what ways can cybersecurity measures future-proof an IT organization?
A4: Strengthening cybersecurity measures protects the organization from evolving cyber threats, ensures the integrity and availability of IT systems, and maintains customer trust, which is essential for long-term success in an increasingly digital world.

Q5: How does adopting a customer-centric approach help in creating a sustainable competitive advantage?
A5: A customer-centric approach aligns IT initiatives with customer needs and expectations, enhancing customer

experiences, increasing loyalty, and differentiating the organization from competitors, thereby creating a sustainable competitive advantage.

Q6: Describe how strategic IT alignment can contribute to creating a sustainable competitive advantage.
A6: Strategic IT alignment ensures that IT strategies support business objectives, allowing organizations to leverage technology for market expansion, product enhancement, and improved customer service, which contributes to a sustainable competitive advantage.

Q7: What is the significance of innovating business models in achieving a competitive advantage?
A7: Innovating business models with technology can open new revenue streams, increase scalability, and offer unique value propositions that set the organization apart from competitors, thereby securing a competitive advantage.

Q8: How does building digital ecosystems enhance an organization's competitive position?
A8: Building digital ecosystems through partnerships and collaborations extends IT capabilities and offerings, enabling the organization to provide more comprehensive solutions and leverage the innovations of partners, thus enhancing its competitive position.

Q9: Why is user experience (UX) important for differentiating in the market?
A9: Investing in UX is vital for differentiation because a superior user experience leads to higher customer satisfaction and loyalty, making it a significant market differentiator that can drive growth and success.

Q10: What role does strategic IT governance play in an organization's success?
A10: Strategic IT governance supports effective decision-

making, prioritizes IT investments based on strategic value, manages risks, and ensures the IT organization is agile, responsive, and aligned with business goals, all of which are key to an organization's success.

Case Study: Digital Transformation at GlobalBank

GlobalBank, a longstanding financial institution, faced increasing competition from fintech startups and recognized the need for digital transformation to stay relevant in the rapidly evolving financial sector. Under the leadership of a visionary CIO, the bank embarked on a comprehensive digital transformation journey.

Initiative 1: Agile and DevOps Implementation
The CIO introduced Agile methodologies and DevOps practices to enhance the speed and efficiency of software development and deployment, aiming to improve the bank's digital services and customer experiences.

Initiative 2: Investment in Emerging Technologies
GlobalBank invested in AI, blockchain, and cloud computing technologies. These investments included developing an AI-driven customer service chatbot, implementing blockchain for secure transactions, and migrating core banking services to the cloud for greater scalability and efficiency.

Initiative 3: Fostering a Culture of Continuous Learning
The CIO established a continuous learning program, offering employees access to online courses, workshops, and certification opportunities in emerging technologies and digital banking trends.

Initiative 4: Strengthening Cybersecurity Frameworks
Recognizing the importance of cybersecurity in the financial industry, GlobalBank revamped its cybersecurity measures, implementing advanced security protocols and conducting regular cybersecurity awareness training for all employees.

Initiative 5: Customer-Centric Digital Services
The bank launched a new mobile banking application with enhanced user experience and personalization features, developed based on customer feedback and behavior analysis.
Outcome
GlobalBank's digital transformation initiatives led to a significant increase in customer satisfaction, a reduction in operational costs, and an improvement in the speed and quality of service delivery. The bank successfully positioned itself as a leader in digital banking, attracting new customers and retaining existing ones.

Case Study Questions

Q1: How did the implementation of Agile and DevOps practices benefit GlobalBank?
Q2: Discuss the strategic importance of GlobalBank's investment in AI, blockchain, and cloud computing.
Q3: How did fostering a culture of continuous learning contribute to GlobalBank's digital transformation?
Q4: Why was strengthening the cybersecurity framework a critical initiative for GlobalBank?
Q5: In what ways did focusing on customer-centric digital services create a competitive advantage for GlobalBank?
Q6: Evaluate the overall impact of the digital transformation initiatives on GlobalBank's market position.
Q7: If you were the CIO of GlobalBank, what additional initiative would you propose to further enhance its digital transformation journey?
Q8: Discuss potential challenges GlobalBank might face in maintaining its digital leadership in the financial sector and how it could address them.

Afterword: Navigating the Evolving Landscape of ITSM

As we conclude our exploration of the intricate tapestry of IT Service Management (ITSM), we find ourselves reflecting on a journey that has seen the field evolve from a supportive backdrop to a leading protagonist in the narrative of digital transformation. This journey, marked by rapid advancements in technology and shifting business paradigms, underscores the resilience and adaptability of ITSM in the face of continuous change.

The evolution of ITSM mirrors the broader evolution of the workplace and technology's role within it. From the initial stages, where IT was seen as a mere facilitator of business operations, to the present day, where IT drives innovation and strategy, ITSM has been pivotal in shaping the digital destiny of organizations. This transformation has not been without challenges, but it has been rewarding, pushing the boundaries of what is possible and redefining the value IT brings to the table.

Looking back, it is clear that the adoption of emerging technologies such as artificial intelligence (AI), machine learning (ML), robotic process automation (RPA), and blockchain has been a game-changer for ITSM. These technologies have not only streamlined operations but have also opened up new avenues for enhancing efficiency, accuracy, and, most importantly, customer satisfaction. The shift towards a more predictive and proactive ITSM model, powered by advanced analytics and predictive insights, is setting a new standard for service delivery.

As we stand on the cusp of a future that promises even more radical transformations, with the potential integration of artificial general intelligence (AGI) and quantum computing, the path forward for ITSM is both exciting and daunting. The promise of autonomous IT operations and the capacity for enhanced decision-making and personalization offered by AGI and quantum computing could revolutionize IT service delivery. However, these advancements also bring forth new challenges and ethical considerations that must be navigated with caution and responsibility.

The journey of ITSM evolution is a testament to the relentless pursuit of excellence and innovation. It is a journey that has not reached its end but is entering a new phase of discovery and exploration. As ITSM professionals, our role in this journey is not just to adapt to changes but to be the catalysts for change, driving the integration of new technologies, advocating for best practices, and fostering a culture of continuous improvement and learning.

As we look to the future, the path forward for ITSM is clear— embrace change, leverage technology for strategic advantage, and continue to place the customer at the center of IT service delivery. The evolution of ITSM is an ongoing process, one that requires resilience, creativity, and a forward-looking mindset. By embracing these qualities, we can ensure that ITSM remains not just relevant but indispensable in the digital era.

In closing, the journey of ITSM evolution is a reflection of our collective commitment to excellence, innovation, and service. It is a journey that celebrates the past, navigates the present, and anticipates the future, always with an eye towards creating value and making a difference in the ever-evolving landscape of technology and business.